unladylike.

'Frank, fun and unapologetically feminist, *Unladylike* will have you chuckling and nodding along in equal measures'—*Vogue*

'*Unladylike* is like reading Judy Blume, Candace Bushnell and Tina Fey all rolled into one. Vaz is brutally and hilariously honest.'—*Newslaundry*

'*Unladylike* is for every woman who dares to be herself in a world telling her otherwise.'—*Verve*

'[U]nlike many "celebrity" authors, Vaz writes lucidly and always has a point to make. There are enough giggles waiting around the corner. I highly recommend you buy your teenage daughter this book for all the early lessons in feminism... Believe me, you'll thank Radhika Vaz for telling it like it is.'—*LiveMint*

'We are hooked to this one, especially since few like Vaz can make gender issues fun.'—*Mid-Day*

'Quirky, uplifting blend of humour, self-introspection, and critical thinking.'—*Firstpost*

'*Unladylike: A Memoir* works as a solid extension of Vaz's comedic mind and as an appendage to her hilarious style.'—*The Hindu*

'Stand-up comics such as Vaz give young women a different template in which to grow up. They tutor us in the art of being a "bad girl" i.e. anyone who doesn't do what society expects of her.'—*Deccan Chronicle*

unladylike.

a memoir

radhika vaz

ALEPH

ALEPH BOOK COMPANY
An independent publishing firm
promoted by **Rupa Publications India**

Published in 2015 by
Aleph Book Company
7/16 Ansari Road, Daryaganj
New Delhi 110 002

Copyright © Radhika Vaz 2015

All rights reserved.

The views and opinions expressed in this book are
the author's own and the facts are as reported by her
which have been verified to the extent possible, and
the publishers are not in any way liable for the same.

No part of this publication may be reproduced,
transmitted, or stored in a retrieval system, in any
form or by any means, without permission in writing
from Aleph Book Company.

ISBN: 978-93-83064-17-5

3 5 7 9 10 8 6 4 2

Printed at Replika Press Pvt. Ltd.

This book is sold subject to the condition that it shall
not, by way of trade or otherwise, be lent, resold, hired
out, or otherwise circulated without the publisher's
prior consent in any form of binding or cover other
than that in which it is published.

*To all the unladies out there
who refuse to be bound
by the rules of femininity.*

CONTENTS

Introduction — ix

THE WONDER YEARS
Who are these two weirdos? — 3
All my life I've simply wanted to belong — 7
Iraqi interlude — 12

I THINK I MAY BE A WOMAN
I want boobs — 23
Becoming a woman — 27
I want a YA — 35
My vagina speaks, does yours? — 41
Scraped knees — 45
Sudden death — 51
I find a new group of friends and porn — 56
If this is virginity, you can have mine — 61
Beauty scout — 69

ROARING TWENTIES
Negotiating singledom — 77
Desperate women do desperate things — 86
Determined to marry — 96

HELLO 'MERICA!
Please let me in — 107
So this is the Land of the Free — 120
White people weather — 139

Living the dream	143
Who will marry this cow?	155

MARRIAGE AND ITS AFTERMATH

City Hall	163
Getting ready to get married	169
Here comes the bride	173
Sexy time	177
The baby question	180
Mother pressure is the new peer pressure	193
Epilogue	197
Acknowledgements	203

INTRODUCTION

As a comedian I can honestly say my face has always been my fortune. One day, after a particularly successful improv scene, my scene partner, Anthony Minto, turned to me and said, *You play ugly so well.* And, because I had made him laugh, I took this as a gigantic compliment. I have always played ugly well; I have a face for it, the same way I have a face for wigs. Any wig, no matter what style or colour, looks like my natural hair. What can I tell you? We all have gifts. These are mine.

Writing a memoir, however, is not. I did not know this when I started writing this book. I thought it would be like writing a show and I thought I would crush it in nine months. It has since been three long years of starts and stops and tantrums and smoking my body weight in hash. It has been humbling. It has been exhilarating. And reading the final draft was so uncomfortable I was almost willing to re-write the whole damn thing. There are things in here I am not proud I said or did, things that are at odds with my feminist beliefs. Was I really this insecure? This desperate for love and attention? Was I this resentful, this annoying, and was I willing to be this vulnerable? I guess so.

I wasn't always like this. I spent many years of my life doing what I could to seem cool, maintain an 'it's all good' exterior. I didn't want anyone to know what I really felt like. I am the girl who has strolled into a nightclub, seen my then boyfling KISSING another girl, said hello to BOTH of them, and then when my horrified friends asked me if I was okay, said I was fine.

Sometimes shock will help you hold on to your dignity. But don't worry, I have since had several opportunities to lose mine. And while I am ashamed to say I took almost every single one, they at least gave me enough material for this book. The best-case scenario is that you will laugh with me at my unsteady progress through life, the worst (from my point of view) is you will see that there is someone right here who is more idiotic than you will ever be. This book is a win-win for you.

People ask me why I do comedy. I do it because I need to vent and I am no longer satisfied with venting to my mum. I do comedy because the expectations laid on women are frightening and I am officially over it. Don't grow hair in your armpits, don't talk about hair in your armpits, don't talk about your armpits. Be perfect all day long, 24/7, don't piss anyone off. Be someone people will like. Look like someone people will like. Are you tall enough? Are you thin enough? Is your skin the right color? Is your vagina tight enough? Is your vagina the right colour?

These are questions that have got to stop haunting us. But how? I don't know. Maybe we can figure this out together.

Now lie back and relax. This will only hurt a little.

I
The Wonder Years

The life and times of an only child.

WHO ARE THESE TWO WEIRDOS?

This is a question I have been asking myself ever since I became acquainted with Surya and Bertie Vaz—my mother and father. I was about four years old when I began to really notice how strange they were and because I was an only child I had to grapple with their weirdness on my own. I couldn't very well ask my friends—hey, who do you suppose those two weirdos are? No, I couldn't because they would have thought that *I* was crazy. And I didn't want them to think that because I already knew they thought I was a freak. That is how you feel if you are an only child growing up in a small town in northern India.

I was the only 'Only' for miles. All the others had at least one sibling and in some cases one to spare. Every time I made a new friend I had to answer the age-old question:

Do you have a brother or sister?
No.
Why not?

Why not, indeed? Hadn't my parents thought about this? Clearly they were aware that this was strange. But they seemed oblivious to the shame and embarrassment that being a freak was causing me. They had been around, they had seen stuff. My dad was one of five—obviously he knew first-hand it could be done. My mother, herself an only child, must have had to deal with the same awkward line of questioning I was being subjected to. Surely she didn't do this on purpose. Or did she? Was she just getting back at the next generation for the crimes committed by the generation before? It was a possibility.

As an Only I felt ganged up on. My parents outnumbered me. It was two against one; I was a minority even in my own home. They had nothing and no one to distract them from keeping an eye on me. Living with them was like living with two detectives on my back at all times. I was screwed! Like all my peers I was constantly doing stuff around the house that I wasn't supposed to be doing. But unlike them I had no one to blame any of my crimes and misdemeanours on. For example: The case of the wax candle—age 5.5.

One day, as I was idly looking for something to destroy, I came across a wax candle. After fidgeting with it for a while and dropping little slivers of wax all over the floor, I discovered it was kind of like a colourless crayon so I searched the house for an appropriate canvas. My parents' wooden closet doors seemed like the perfect place—dark wood, smooth, glossy and unmarred. I drew what I thought resembled a pair of cowboy boots, a tree, and several other works of art. I took hours over it and was pleased with the final effect.

Later the same day—when I had completely forgotten about all this—my mother found my handiwork.

Radhika.

Yes.

Come here, please.

Whenever my mother was polite to me I knew something was wrong. As I walked into her room and saw her standing in front of the closet I remembered.

Did you do this?

Why couldn't these two people have had just one more kid? Just one more, then I could have immediately blamed it on someone else. I had seen this work for my playmates. One sibling would blame it on the other, making the parents so sick and tired of trying to figure out which one to believe that they would just yell at both of them and then let it go. I was positive she was going to smack me.

Ahem. Did you do this?

No.

My mother was frighteningly cool.

Really?

Yes.

Because I had the under-developed mind of a child I actually thought that she believed me. And thinking I was in the clear I decided to draw her attention to a few of the works that I quite frankly thought were ahead of their time.

I wonder what this drawing is, I pondered aloud, as I drew her eye to one of the still lifes.

Ah it's a pair of cowboy boots, I declared, thus answering my own question.

See it has a star on the side and spurs—these are the spurs. Oh and look at this one.

My mother stepped aside so I could proceed with the art lecture, and taking her silence for encouragement I dug my grave even deeper.

So you have absolutely no idea who did this?

I was brimming with confidence now.

None!

Go get me some soap and water, please.

I couldn't believe it! She didn't even ask me to clean it, she just did it herself. I got out of there before she changed her mind.

I could never understand this beautiful woman. Sometimes she looked like she was thinking, 'Somebody please take this pest off my hands', and sometimes she was a patient, loving, maternal figure. I like to think she was just trying to even out the odds for me. She knew that if she'd had more than one child to look after, it was likely I would have gotten away more often, and so every now and then she let me. Either that or I grew up with a schizophrenic mother. I have no idea—like I said, I had no one to help me understand my situation or my parents.

ALL MY LIFE I'VE SIMPLY WANTED TO BELONG

My dad is ethnically from Goa but was born and raised in Bombay. My mum is ethnically half Andhra and half Kodava but was born in Jamshedpur and raised between there and boarding school in Darjeeling. I was born in Bombay and because my dad was in the air force I was raised in Pathankot, Secunderabad, Ghaziabad, Bareilly, Udhampur, Iraq, Wellington, Hasimara, Bangalore and went to boarding school near Ooty. Every single conversation that involved me telling people where I was from went something like this:

Where are you from?
Hasimara.
Where is that?
West Bengal.
You don't look Bengali.
Well, my dad's from Goa.
Oh, so you are Goan.
Well—my mum's half Andhra and half Kodava.
Okay, so where are you from?

'I don't fucking know' would have been the correct answer. I was from nowhere and everywhere at the same time. Right through school and college most of my friends could define themselves in a word or at the very most a short sentence. *I am Malayali* or *I am Kashmiri* or *I am a Marwari from Guwahati.* They were so sure of where they came from, where they belonged and, most important of all, where they stood when the lines were drawn—which in India they most inevitably will be. I remember a conversation between two classmates.

Where are you from?
Baroda.
Gujarati? You don't look.
Of course I am—pure Gujarati.

Pure! No argument. Case closed. She was pure silk, I was an unknown polyester blend.

When I was five, my dad was posted to Udhampur, a small town in J&K and as there was no family accommodation available, my parents and I lived in civilian territory instead of at the air force base where my dad worked. My folks had rented a small house at the top of a hill. The only way to get to our house was via a steep incline of steps that began at the main road and ended at our boundary wall. There was no road for a car or scooter. I remember this particularly well because of the frantic sprint down that my mum and I had to undertake every morning so I could catch the school bus. And then of course the climb back up every afternoon. Despite this, our location was considered central because we were close to the main bazaar area from where I once stole an orange, my first and last foray into shoplifting. While Udhampur itself did not make much of an impression on me, our neighbours there sure did.

There was just one other house on the hill and it belonged to our landlord—a large and friendly Sardar family who can best be described as salt-of-the-earth. Their house was much larger than ours, two storeys high and home to three generations of people. Despite living in a town they had managed to sustain the flavour of village life and this was evidenced by the herd of buffaloes they owned. These beasts lived in the sawmill compound right by the main road where our landlord parked his trucks and where my dad parked his blue Standard Herald, this fleet forming a sort of welcoming committee to whoever climbed the hill.

Soon after we moved there, my mother, wanting me out of her hair, dragged me to the neighbour's house to help me make friends and this is how I met Roopinder. She was the oldest of the gazillion kids that lived there and closest to my age. She was also the tallest and I immediately wanted her to be my friend.

I adored Roopinder. No, that would be an understatement, I *worshipped* her. She was most definitely the leader of the pack and like sheep we would follow her everywhere she went. I liked everything about her and now that I think about it, it was around this time that I must have subconsciously begun to form an idea of what the perfect Indian girl should be. I was looking for a benchmark to measure myself to see how I was holding up. Roopinder became my prototype; to me she was the norm and if I wanted to fit in I would have to basically be her.

Unlike my family, Roopinder's had deep roots, and like a banyan tree they were out there for the world to see. They were Punjabi and, although born and raised in J&K for several generations—they were purebred. Everything they did went back to their heritage. While we ate eggs and toast for breakfast and drank tea, Roopinder's family ate paranthas and drank lassi, lassi they made from dahi, which was made from milk that they got from their buffaloes. And every summer holiday they went back to their village. I didn't have a village; when I had summer holidays I went to Bombay or Bangalore to visit my grandparents, neither of whom were actually even from Bombay or Bangalore. I never knew if Roopinder was at all curious about my summer vacay, but I sure as hell was curious about hers.

I would hang out with Roopinder and her endless number of siblings and cousins as much as I could and during my association with them I began to notice certain things, one being that Roopinder's family spoke Punjabi to each other and Hindi to 'outsiders' like me. Punjabi was the language they chose to communicate with the ones they really loved and were bound to. I envied Roopinder and her clan, not for their binding love but for what was effectively a secret code. This was not the case with my family. In a country of a thousand languages and an equal variety of dialects, we at the Vaz household spoke to one another in English. My parents' (so-called) mixed marriage had left us no choice.

The problem with my parents wasn't just the speaking of English; my dad liked all kinds of strange English music as well. All I ever got to hear was jazz, disco and American bubblegum pop. Unfortunately the songs that were popular with my age group were either Hindi nursery rhymes or Bollywood tunes. And so while Roopinder and her ilk belted out the entire soundtrack of *Bobby* and *Sholay* and other blockbuster films from the 70s, I sat silent and alone in the knowledge that I was probably the only kid in the entire state who knew the words to Connie Francis' 'Lipstick on Your Collar'. A song about a boy who had lied to his girl, who wore baby-pink lipstick, about going out for a soda-pop but instead was kissing that tramp Mary Jane who wore whorish red lipstick.

Because my friends did not either understand or appreciate my tunes, and I prefer to believe it was the language barrier and not my complete lack of talent, I would watch while they sang, a plight that only an attention-desiring five-year-old can relate to. I would then go home and subject both my parents to renditions of 'Lipstick' and Ms Francis' other hit 'Stupid Cupid'. I would have preferred a larger audience—much like the one Roopinder catered to—but I had no choice. I knew my friends weren't trying to exclude me on purpose, it was just the way the chips happened to fall. They were on the inside, I was on the outside and all I ever wanted from that point on was to be on the inside.

The only upside of singing to my parents was the technology. My dad had a set of mikes that he could plug into his amp and actually record stuff onto cassette tapes and so I would have them sit through my two-song repertoire insisting that they tape these performances as well.

What made this infinitely worse for them to endure was that while the tape was running we had no way of playing the Connie Francis record as an accompaniment (karaoke style). These tapings were of me going hammer and tongs with no recorded music to drown out my complete lack of musical ability. As I pounded Connie's melodies into the ground, one note at a time, my mother and father would sit straight-faced, encouraging me with an occasional smile and at the end I would accept their applause and admiration in the off-hand fashion that a true rock-star reserves for her sluttiest groupies.

As soon as the concert was over I would have my dad play the recording back for us and I was always devastated that I sounded nothing like my American idol.

I'm pretty sure both parents were on the verge of telling me exactly why it was that I did not and never would come close to sounding like the original but they kept it to themselves. Eventually I would get bored and fuck off to my room to torture my doll and stuffed monkey—my two companions who, thankfully, did not speak at all.

IRAQI INTERLUDE

In 1979 when I was six my parents informed me that we would be moving to a foreign country for two years. Up until then the only foreign country I had heard anything about was the United States of America. As a young pilot with the Indian air force my father had lived there while he learnt to fly fighter planes. So when they told me we were going to a foreign country, I assumed we were off to America and I was thrilled. Maybe I would finally meet Connie Francis?

Naturally, when we disembarked in Baghdad I was more than a little surprised. I was expecting to be greeted by a sea of blue eyes and blond hair, but instead I was confronted by folks who looked a lot like me. By the time we made it to our hotel I was moved to ask my mother wtf was up.

Where are we?
In Iraq.
But I thought we were going to a foreign country.
This is a foreign country.
I thought we were going to America.
We are not going to America. Now sit quietly, I'm jetlagged.
What's jetlagged?
Jetlagged is when you are tired and fed-up.

A few days later we left Baghdad for our final destination. We were one of many Indian families that would end up scattered across three Iraqi air force bases. My parents and I joined four other families on the smallest one, the K2 airbase, located about an hour from Tikrit, in the northern part of the country. There was a time when I'd have had to explain all this but today everyone knows that this is where Saddam Hussein was from.

All five families were housed together in a block of beige flats surrounded by absolutely nothing but miles of beige sand. I had never ever seen so much sand or so much empty horizon in my life. Our building was literally in the middle of nowhere. There was nothing there. No people, no shops, no homes, no trees, no signs of life whatsoever. The only other building of note as far as I could tell was a massive industrial structure a few miles away. This was the K2 oil-pipeline pumping station that the airbase had been designed to protect. It was a spectacular sight, especially at night when it was lit up like a Christmas tree. But that was it. Developmentally, K2 looked like one big afterthought.

The other air force bases were much cooler than ours. They had swimming pools and club houses and all kinds of neat stuff. And it wasn't surprising—they were located in places that had actual names. We were living in a place that was so shitty it didn't have a name.

Ma?
Yes?
Is there a K1?
Who knows?

The shock of being in this remote and rather bleak place was quickly softened by two things. The first: because we were in the boondocks of an Arabic-speaking nation the only school system available to us was Arabic medium. And so for the entire duration of my stay I did not attend school. To say that these were the two most blissful years of my childhood would be an understatement. Some of the other air force bases had more industrious mothers who had gotten together and home-schooled their offspring—thankfully, none of these schoolmarms had made it to K2, and so I was allowed to run about like a wild animal all day long. I had two friends—Sher Singh and Zora Singh, two siblings my age, and our entire day was playtime. We would go home for our feed and water and then go back to doing absolutely nothing constructive.

The other thing that made my life worth living was television. We had not owned a TV until then so just having one was a thrill, but the truly brilliant part was that in those days the Iraqis were broadcasting all the major American TV shows. I watched as much TV as humanly possible, including several shows that were clearly meant for adults. I devoutly followed *Little House on the Prairie*, *Eight is Enough*, *Love Boat*, and what would become my favourite show—*Dallas*, thanks to which I developed my first crush and fell hard for the baddest bad boy on the show, JR. I knew Bobby was the one everyone liked—he was cute and far nicer than JR—but even at a young age I found there was something attractive about a man whose smile made you forget that he was entirely capable of sticking a knife in your back. Lucky for me, my mother was not one to worry about what was and wasn't appropriate TV viewing for children and so I came to watch American people kill, steal and have sexual relations with reckless, soap-operatic abandon.

I thought that my life was complete, until a year later when, thanks to some of my aunties, I got to watch my first ever Miss Universe pageant. Beauty competitions are to little girls what porn is to little boys. The proceedings are not in our immediate future but we know that at some point they can be. I could see myself parading about in a swimsuit and a sash. And so that night my fate was sealed. I knew what I wanted to be when I grew up: a blond-haired, blue-eyed woman called Shawn Weatherly (1980's Miss USA) who won the Miss Universe title.

Ma?
Yes?
I want blue eyes and blond hair.
I see.

How can I get blue eyes and blond hair?
Maybe if you wish for it hard enough.

With my birthday fast approaching I decided this is what I'd do. I would stop fervently wishing for the Lego set and mini-vacuum cleaner I had been wanting and concentrate all my efforts on changing the colour of my hair and eyes.

Traditional Indian parents make their children the centre of their universe. A child's birthday party is practically sacred and the child's happiness is central on that day. Anything the child wants, it gets. I woke up on mine with black hair and black eyes. Clearly, I wasn't getting off to a good start. But I had also asked for a few other things. For starters, I had requested that pink streamers be used to spell out 'Happy Birthday Radhika' on the big blank wall in the living room. I had seen Zora's dad do that for him on his birthday. My dad was put in charge of doing this. What I ended up with was 'Happy B'day RV'.

Full names and full words are for babies. You are a grown-up now.

And surely I was, judging from the full bar that he had lovingly spent most of the day setting up. That was the year I realized that my birthday was just an opportunity for my parents and their friends to have a good time. Once the tedious cake-cutting, song-singing and picture-taking was over and done with—as far as they were concerned, so was my birthday. Now it was their turn to enjoy themselves and they did.

My dad's generation of Indian fathers had a fairly hands-off approach to child rearing. If they had a boy they were usually brought in when major disciplinary action was required. If they had a girl then the role was that of protector, provider and most important, the pamperer. Normal fathers treated their daughters like princesses—daddy's girls. I didn't and still do not have that relationship with my dad and here is why—Iraq. Iraq was where my dad was forced to interact with me more than he ever had. Not knowing exactly what to do, he raised me the way he might have had I been a boy, and sometimes I wonder if he went too far.

Once, during one of the many adult parties we kids were allowed to attend, mostly because there was nowhere to leave us, my friend Deepak Sukrutaraj and I kept begging our respective chain-smoking fathers to let us have a cigarette. Most parents would have said a firm NO, or perhaps been driven to do some soul-searching in regard to their habit. Not these two. They decided to let us smoke.

Breathe it in deeply, were the last words I heard before I almost blacked out from a coughing fit.

In general, my dad didn't get me, but he did get one thing. My need for speed. Upon arriving in Iraq all the other dads had gone off and bought responsible-looking cars with four doors; mine bought a two-door Toyota Celica, a sporty little thing that he loved almost as much as I did. When my mother had had enough of me and my barrage of questions on how I could convert myself into a white American, she would send my dad off to entertain me. My father would take me to the runway at the airbase. Once we got there he would let me sit on his lap—a cigarette burning brightly in his mouth—and he would let me steer the car. We would go up and down the runway with me squealing 'faster, faster' and my dad happily obliging. We would take sharp turns and brake suddenly, and all kinds of fun things that a six-year-old with no concept of death would find greatly amusing. Needless to say neither he nor I had a seatbelt on.

About eighteen months into our stay there, the war between Iraq and Iran broke out. While this was not explicitly told to us kids we were warned not to go to the air force base on our cycles anymore. Things were a bit of a drag until one day Sher Singh, Zora Singh and I came upon a man digging a long, deep ditch outside our building. He patiently explained with what little English he knew that this was a trench, and told us why we needed it, and what would befall us should we not get in the trench when the time came. I did not know this then but the beautiful Christmas tree-like oil pumping station that I had so admired was now a major target for an air strike, and with it so were we.

As soon as we collected all this information we went off to inform the rest of the crew and for the remainder of the day played Iraqis versus Iranians. Then life got real exciting. There were several trial air raids, practice sessions to see how fast the building could be evacuated—if you had seen us running from the building to the trenches you would have thought we were off to Disneyland because that is how much fun we were having. All the fun came to an end of course when an actual air raid managed to hit the airstrip on which my dad and I used to practice our driving, and a few weeks later we were evacuated to Baghdad.

Moving from K2 to Baghdad was like moving from the moon to New York City. For one thing there were people there. All the Indians from the three air bases had been evacuated at more or less the same time and so we were all shoved together in one big building. The downside was I didn't have my own room anymore but the upside was I could finally play with girls. No more dinky cars and Lego sets. Now, much to my delight, I was surrounded with dolls. It was doll houses, doll clothes, doll tea sets, and doll tea parties all day long.

When it rains it pours and I made yet another female friend. The house next door to our building belonged to an Iraqi family and our balcony afforded me an unfettered view of it. They had a long walled but oddly roofless passageway that led from the road all the way to the back of the house and I could observe all the passageway activities at leisure. I took special interest in them because they had two children, a boy and a girl, who I estimated to be about my size and so I figured we would have plenty in common. I was particularly drawn to the girl. Unlike me, she went to school, had a uniform and school bag, and along with her other female classmates had to tie a scarf over her head. I didn't realize this was a religious requirement—I thought it was cosmetic and I liked it a lot.

I appropriated one of my mother's dupattas and after wrapping myself in it I went off to play with her. She spoke no English, I spoke no Arabic but we managed to make ourselves understood. She taught me a few Arabic words—numbers from one to ten. And she also taught me a phrase that was popular on the street in those days.

Saddam Hussein Zain. Khomeini Zidan Meeuzain.

(Saddam Hussein is great, Khomeini—not so great.)

She and her brother had been taught this in school and they had to chant it every day while walking to and from school with their other classmates. Quite often if I had managed to wake up early enough I would grab my dupatta and rush off to chant with them.

Saddam Hussein Zain. Khomeini Meeuzain. Saddam Hussein Zain. Khomeini Zidan Meeuzain. Saddam Hussein Zain. Khomeini Meeuzain.

I had to tear myself away at the main street because that was as far as I was allowed to go. This chant helped me bond with her family as well. They must have been delighted to see my fanatical appreciation for their great leader and I would bask in the glow of their approval.

No problem, no problem.

They assured my mother when she apologized on some evenings when I may have overstayed my welcome.

During the day when she went to school I would devote myself to a newfound passion. I was done with *Dallas* and was now into *The Adventures of Flash Gordon*. I convinced myself I was Dale—Flash's one true love. She wore a costume that was remarkably close in design to a bikini and so I lobbied for one of my own. My mother complied with this wish and I wound up with an orange string bikini that I paired with green rain boots, and my mother's trusty dupatta was now fashioned into a cape.

Radhika.
Yes ma.
You can't wear this outfit outside.
Why?
Because you might catch a cold.
But it's not cold.
Well, you still can't wear it outside.

Even then I knew perfectly well that there was absolutely no point putting a costume together if no one was going to see it.

Can I at least wear it on the balcony?
May I?
May I wear it on the balcony?
Magic word.

What was the problem with this woman.

May I wear it on the balcony, please?
All right.

I rushed to the balcony pretending I was in a spaceship and off to help Flash fight Ming the Merciless. I was busy hurtling through the outer limits of space when I suddenly saw my friend marching back from school. I waved frantically to her and we began chanting.

Saddam Hussein Zain. Khomeini Zidan Meeuzain. Saddam Hussein Zain. Khomeini Zidan Meeuzain. Saddam Hussein Zain. Khomeini Zidan Meeuzain.

But life wasn't all a bed of roses. On occasion we would fight. Maybe one of us had inadvertently dissed the other. Or maybe she hung on to my beloved Barbie for longer than the time I had decided was permissible. On those days she would keep to the street directly in front of her home and I would keep to the street directly in front of our building. We were twenty feet apart at the most but we refused to acknowledge each other. I would watch her out of the corner of my eye as she enjoyed a game of hopscotch, clearly not missing me one bit and it would drive me mad. I considered starting a round of fisticuffs but I knew my mother would kill me. But if I couldn't push her, pull her hair, or smack her, how in the world was I to get her attention.

And then it hit me. I turned to her and yelled:

Saddam Hussein Moooooooozain. Khomeini ZAIN.

She stopped what she was doing and spun around to face me. The gravity of what I had said began to sink in along with the realization that she could definitely give me a much harder ass-kicking than I could possibly give her. I turned on my cowardly heel and sprinted the twenty feet to the foyer of our building. When I turned around she had not only *not* followed me but she had gone right back to the hopscotch game I had previously interrupted. I was infuriated.

Saddam Hussein Moooooooozain. Khomeini ZAIN.

I screeched. No response.

Saddam Hussein Moooooooozain. Khomeini ZAIN.

I trilled. Still no response from her although I had now managed to attract the attention of all the Iraqi adults in the vicinity. Feeling very foolish and very angry I stomped off upstairs where I kept vigilance on her and her family from our balcony for the rest of the evening.

The next day I awoke. It was almost time for her to leave for school; I grabbed my dupatta and rushed downstairs. It was only when I saw her standing there waiting for her friends that I remembered my idiotic behaviour from the previous day. I froze in my tracks as she turned to me—and then she just smiled. We marched to the end of the street joyfully singing Saddam Hussein's praises.

At the end of the day little girls don't give a crap about who's Zain and who's Meeuzain—they just want to play. But adult life took over ours and a short while later we left for the relative safety of Kuwait from where we would eventually set sail for India.

II

I Think I May Be a Woman

Teen Rad aka Anil Kapoor's hair double.

I WANT BOOBS

A few years after our return from Iraq, my parents decided that I needed to be raised with values and a work ethic and, recognizing their own shortcomings, put me in boarding school. I was ten years old when I joined 700 other kids at Lawrence School, Lovedale. Getting me to agree to go there had been an easy sell; I had always been fascinated by the idea of boarding schools. My mother had kept me enthralled with stories of her own experience at Mt. Hermon in Darjeeling and I was a devout reader of Enid Blyton's Mallory Towers series. And so I didn't need much convincing. I was just dying to go. That is, until I got there. Let's just say that the beautiful hundred-year-old buildings, the damp misty weather and the towering eucalyptus trees were all very well in theory. In practice, while it did conjure up a most romantic atmosphere, it also depressed the shit out of me. I was miserably homesick.

To add to my woes, the Girls' School, which housed the 120 female students (talk about being in the minority), was run by a collection of women straight out of *Oliver Twist*. The two that stand out in my memory are Mrs Krishnaprabhu, a rotund, solid citizen who had lost her husband years before and so we knew had no heart, and Ms Shreedhar, our ancient and perpetually irritated Math teacher, who also moonlighted as housemistress to a bunch of us. I was always in one or the other's bad books. As the years went by I made friends, got over my homesickness and began focusing on far more pressing matters. I was a teenager now and my biggest fear at the time was that I was going to grow up to be a man.

As odd as this may sound, I spent a great deal of my time being secretly suspicious of my gender, and with very good reason. After an unfortunate attack of lice during my first year at school, my mother had shorn my hair within an inch of my scalp.

She looks just like Audrey Hepburn. My father had lied without actually looking at me when he said this.

With my short hair and rail-thin body, when in a dress, I looked less like Ms Hepburn and more like a teenage drag queen. It was clear to me that I was missing a vital element of womanhood—breasts. Perhaps I would not have missed them as much if I had been raised in a flat-chested country like Japan or China, but having been raised Indian and grown up feeling every woman had big, bountiful boobs simply led to a major case of boob-envy, an affliction that I have to live with to this day.

When I was eight, my parents bought me my first Barbie doll— 'Ballerina Barbie'. I immediately locked myself in the bathroom, ripped her tutu off and subjected her to a gynaecological exam that would have landed any doctor in jail. I would stare at my bony chest in the mirror and hope that one day I too would have what she did. I did not hold out much hope though because I had already spent a lot of my time locked in bathrooms trying on my mother's bras which is what got me even more worried about my future. She wasn't that well endowed herself. I saw the other mothers parading about showing off their cleavages and I felt bad because as a family we were thoroughly unimpressive. And now, here in the dorms, where we were all constantly changing in front of one another, the absence of boobage was only magnified by how present it was on everyone else.

With the exception of a few other unfortunates *all* my classmates had boobs, and bras into which they would put these boobs every day. In the 80s we didn't have trainer bras in India, so there was nothing that could help a flat-chested girl feel like one of the crowd. I had to wear—I hate even having to think about it—a child-sized wife-beater like the boys did. And to make sure I never lost these valuable items, my mother had helpfully embroidered **R. VAZ** in red on the chest.

No matter how hard I fought to ignore my obvious inadequacies they followed me everywhere. During bath time I would gaze admiringly, and as covertly as possible, at the girls who had breasts, something I still do. I would inspect how their towels would lift gloriously where mine fell flat. I would be rudely jolted out of my reverie by the sharp voice of one of the seniors I had been staring at.

Radhika Vaz! Eyes off deck!

In Math class as Ms Shreedhar waxed on and on about integers and rational numbers and polynomials, I sat there staring enviously at her breasts, or at least what I assumed would be the general area of her breasts. Being a conservative Indian lady she did a pretty good job of keeping them hidden from view by wearing a cardigan, a shawl, and then wrapping her sari around her like a cape. Ms Shreedhar was a superhero of sorts and one of her most finely honed skills was being able to detect who was and who wasn't paying attention.

Radhika Vaz! Look at her—sitting there, staring into space.

It wasn't like I was miserable about this all day every day, but now and then something would happen to remind me of my inadequacies. Like the time I had to wear my Sunday kit for the Christmas choir. Our 'Sunday' kit was actually never worn on Sunday—it was a rather sexy pencil skirt and blazer set that was worn for a variety of events that required formality, and the yearly Christmas pageant was one such occasion. I hated that jacket. It did nothing but highlight all that was missing. I sneaked off to the washroom where I first shoved a pair of socks into my shirt. This gave the impression that I had recently had a pretty serious boob job. Nope—it was too unrealistic. I then tried stuffing increasing amounts of notebook paper. The problem with paper is that it isn't smooth and so I ended up with what looked like lumpy boobs. Eventually I gave up and spent the whole evening mired in insecurity.

There was also the time on the games field. All the girls wore white shirts for sporting activities, and one day as we were playing hockey, and as all my teammates were bouncing about in their bras, it began to rain. It was an all-out downpour and in minutes it became a wet t-shirt contest. My top was soaked and the R.VAZ was glowing through like a neon sign alerting the world to my shortcomings.

Everyone ran to take cover in the gym. Where ALL the boys were! I was mortified—now the whole school would know that I did not wear a bra. They had probably guessed this but now it would be confirmed. The boys in my class had been making fun of me for years and now they would have even more ammunition. I had to find a way out. As luck would have it, Vinita Aggarwal, one of the most stacked seniors happened to be wearing a sweater over her shirt.

Vinita, I'm not feeling very well, I bluffed, *may I borrow your sweater, please?*

If I had been blessed with boobage like hers I would have been happy to take my sweater off. Not Vinita. She looked at me like I was insane.

If I take it off you can see everything! My shirt is wet and there are guys in the gym!

Exactly! I wanted to yell, wasn't that the whole point of having boobs? For boys to look at? What else were we going to do with our boobs anyway? I could not understand her response, and I never forgave her.

BECOMING A WOMAN

I became a woman in Calcutta. Well, I probably became a woman on the flight into Calcutta but my womanliness was brought to my attention in a toilet at Calcutta's Dum Dum Airport. I might have learned of my transition earlier but, back then, I avoided urinating in aircraft toilets because I was terrified of being sucked into the commode and flung into space. My dad was on the flight with me and, being a pilot, appeared to be irritated at having a child who didn't have the balls to use the lavatory on an airplane.

Even if the flush suction were that strong you wouldn't fit through the hole. When my dad is very annoyed with stupidity he tries to reason with it.

What did he know? Had he even watched *Airport*?

I was also afraid of being attacked by a shark while swimming in the deep end of a pool, something else he was deeply unsympathetic towards.

Okay, just hurry up.

My dad hated being put off his schedule by my unfounded phobias. However, due to reasons outside his control, and mine, I was stuck with my dad and he was stuck with the chore of taking me to Calcutta.

By this time my parents, who had made a habit of living in places no one who was anyone had heard of, were stationed in Hasimara on the border of Bhutan and West Bengal. While I am sure Hasimara has many redeeming features, as a sulky, bored teenager, I chose to focus on the leeches that thrived there, thanks to the perennially damp weather. I suppose I should have been grateful I didn't live there full-time and only visited twice a year for the holidays, but even that was too much for me. For one thing, it took what felt like serious hardship just to get there.

The first leg of my journey had involved a lot of vomiting. Lovedale was high up in the Nilgiri hills and the closest major train station was in Mettupalayam. To get there we had to take a bus ride down a very steep hill that included thirty-six of the most treacherous hairpin bends I have ever experienced. It was like being on a rollercoaster for three hours non-stop, a rollercoaster commandeered by a speed-junkie who hated children and wanted to see us all throw up our insides and be miserable. From there it was an overnight train to Chennai, where we boarded the Coromandel Express that would take us up the eastern coast to Calcutta. While the train was described as an 'express', and while it was supposed to cover the 1,662-kilometre distance in less than thirty-six hours, the truth was it usually took at least two days to reach its destination. Most kids would disembark in Calcutta but my voyage was far from over. I had to go further east, and for that I had a one-hour flight from Calcutta to Bagdogra, followed by a six-hour drive to look forward to. And now I was making this ghastly journey in reverse.

Because I wasn't a 'local', I had just one friend in Hasimara—Sanjay Pandit, a boy my age who enjoyed cricket and violent films, two activities I loathed. Moreover, it was clear that the only reason he was being friendly was because his mum was pals with my mum. On top of all this, my parents themselves were virtual strangers—all teenagers face this problem but living away from them eight months of the year made it more than just a figure of speech. I also considered them to be the two most boring, un-cool humans on the planet and being forced to spend my summer holidays with them, Sanjay Pandit, and the leeches in this hideous hick town was a fate worse than death.

Which is why I was smugly pleased to have unintentionally upset my father.

I'll wait there. He pointed out a snack counter that was serving all kinds of disgusting, deep-fried offerings.

It is a fact that the harder one needs to pee, the longer the line outside the toilet will be. After what felt like an eternity it was my turn to go. I went in, pulled my pants down and there staring back at me was a reddish-brown blotch of femininity.

I knew of girls who had wept fearfully at the sight of their first period. Not me. Unlike aircraft toilets and swimming pool sharks, this was something I had been looking forward to for a very long time. I was a month shy of my fourteenth birthday and, in my mind, this was an apparently early birthday pressie from Mother Nature, a promise from her that despite outwardly appearances I was indeed going to grow up to become a lady. While my under-developed chesticles did nothing for my sagging self-confidence, my severely delayed menstrual cycle had only helped make things worse. While all around me my friends blossomed into women who menstruated with great regularity I lay awake at night nervously knowing that it was only a matter of time before my voice broke and my balls dropped.

It was awful. Every other morning one of my dorm mates would wake up and gasp that her period had started. We referred to the monthly cycle as 'chums' and someone or other was always going on about her 'chums' and the accompanying 'chum cramps'. They would merrily interrupt hockey practice to inform us of how bad it was, clutching their sides and doubling over with pain. All the other girls would be most sympathetic because they knew what it felt like. As everyone crowded around offering advice on how best to deal with the situation I would try to be part of the gang nodding my head and parroting anything that the other girls said.

Why don't you sit down, Nancy, you'll feel better.

Yes, Nancy, sit down—sit down at once, I chirped, while filing away for future reference the fact that sitting down was preferable to standing up if Aunt Flo' were visiting.

Is it your second day? That's always the worst.

Yes, the second day—the second day is the worst, the very worst! This was news to me but I wasn't going to let on.

Does anyone have an Asprin or a Disprin? Why any of us would be carrying pharmaceutical drugs to hockey practice was beyond me but the girl asking had big tits and probably started chumming at the age of four, so I followed her lead.

Yes, goddammit, does anyone have any Asprin or Disprin—can't you see Nancy is in pain?! Help us, please!

Secretly, I hated Nancy and didn't care how much pain she was in. In fact I hated everyone who had their chums and suspected that they were showing off anytime they mentioned it. Then and there I promised God that if She granted me the gift of my chums, unlike the weak-minded nitwits I was surrounded by, I wouldn't complain about any of it. I would bear my womanliness with pride and without modern medication.

This feeling that somehow I was being left out on purpose persisted, and with no godly intervention in sight, I figured that the only thing that would make me feel better would be if I pretended I had come of age. I had done this all my life—pretending to have brothers, sisters, friends from foreign lands, exotic pets, so why not this? The only trouble was, I had none of the props with which to pretend, none of accoutrements that went with womanhood, namely the sanitary towel or the 'ST' as we lovingly call pads in India. Most girls in my age range had a pack of these things that their mothers had given them 'just in case'. My mother probably took one look at me and knew I would never get my period and so she had not even bothered. I thought about putting some of my precious pocket money towards the purchase of some STs but it was a massive investment worth six egg-cheese rolls at our snack shop. Needless to say, my stomach won.

Things were looking decidedly bleak until one fine day my friend Preeti informed me that she was going home for a week as her grandmother had died. Because she couldn't possibly take all her things with her on this trip, and because we didn't get large closet spaces to store our stuff, Preeti asked if I wouldn't mind stashing some of her clothes and other valuables in my suitcase. I happily agreed mainly because I had my eyes on her Nike sneakers. So it was a fortuitous surprise when I discovered that in addition to her cool keds Preeti had left behind her pack of Comfit Sanitary Towels!

On the totem pole of sanitary pads I knew that Comfit was the least desirable. They were the cheapest and the packaging was tacky and old-fashioned. And my mother, the litmus test for all things infra-dig, used them. But beggars can't be choosers so I grabbed all her stuff, hustled her off into the waiting taxi and then rushed to my dorm to stow everything in my bag. Everything except the sanitary pads—these were left on display in my locker for all to see. I will say one thing for Comfit—what it lacked in brand appeal it more than made up for in flash. Unlike its more conservative sisters—Stayfree and Carefree—the packaging was anything but subtle; with its little blue flowers on a bright yellow backdrop, it positively screamed 'property of a menstruating woman'.

Much to my disappointment no one paid any heed. I had been anticipating some sort of acknowledgement but none was forthcoming. So, I decided on a slightly more aggressive strategy. I made a big show of rearranging my closet, heaping all my gear on the dorm floor, making doubly sure it was in everyone's way with the Comfit packet perched conspicuously on top of the pile. That didn't work either. I even left the package carelessly on my bed, my desk and on the windowsill. All I managed to achieve was a yelling from one of the prefects for being untidy.

In the end I contented myself by opening up the package and conducting a meticulous inspection of the pads, the accompanying belt to keep them in place, and the diagrammatic instructions on how they were to be worn. And when I finally got bored with that, I used the pads. The sensation was akin to how I felt when I would secretly try on my mother's bras—ill-fitting, awkward, but oh so grown-up! For a few days I lived the dream, hoping that the pad had somehow informed my gait and overall demeanour enough to signal to my peers that I was now one of them.

When Preeti returned I handed her back all her things, minus the STs, and luckily for me she was too distraught by her grandmother's passing to notice. A few weeks later the term ended and we were herded home. The holidays passed without a chum in sight although by this time I had resigned myself to the horror that at some point my body was going to suddenly sprout a penis. And so you can only imagine my relief when in Dum Dum Airport I realized this would not come to pass.

This was the beginning of the rest of my life! I couldn't wait to get back to school and moan and groan along with all my friends about the unfairness of being a woman, now that I was absolutely sure I was one. I sat there feeling incredibly mature when it dawned upon me that the only person I had to share this good news with was my dad. With no STs and no money of my own I was going to have to enlist his assistance. This realization quickly turned into fury against my mother. Unlike the other mothers who had clearly thought all this through, mine had basically left me to fend for myself. I sat there, crouched in the stall, with my undies around my ankles, plotting my next move.

First, I had to stem the flow as it were and so I made do with a pile of toilet tissue the height of the Eiffel Tower. I then shuffled back to the terminal looking like Clint Eastwood after a very long horseback ride, hoping that by the time I came face-to-face with my father I would have some idea of how I was going to broach the subject. When I found him he was leafing through a newspaper with one hand and stuffing a mutton samosa into his face with the other.

Pa.

There you are.

My—periods have started. The direct approach.

A lengthy silence ensued as my father considered this while simultaneously consuming the rest of his samosa.

Did your mother tell you anything about this? He finally managed.

What a stupid question I thought but did not say. If my mother had told me anything about anything I wouldn't need to enlist his help now, would I?

No, but I know everything. I just need pads. Thank god for Preeti and my fake period.

Excellent—come with me, I think there is a chemist somewhere around here. He had stopped making eye contact with me by this point.

We went along to the chemist, him rushing ahead and me waddling along behind him desperately trying to keep Le Tour Eiffel in place. Once there, he nodded to me indicating that I should pick out whatever I needed and that was when I was able to see the silver lining of my situation—thank god I was with my father and not my budget-conscious, bore of a mother. She would have surely forced those disgusting Comfit STs upon me. But with my dad I was free to choose and so I did. *Stayfree with wings. Two packs please.*

I spent the next few weeks in a state of unimaginable ecstasy. My body had taken a big step in the right direction. I discovered that I was one of those girls who never suffered chum cramps or bloating and not just that but my chest began showing some signs of swelling—very, very tiny signs, for sure, but signs nonetheless.

Life was good!

Of course the moment something starts to go well you can be sure something bad will happen to balance it all out and I had to contend with one side effect of my chums I had not accounted for. Body hair. The stuff had begun to manifest itself a few years earlier but now it was getting positively luxuriant. And to my dismay this was probably one area in which I was far ahead of the girls in my class—and some of the boys as well. This realization brought me right back to square one—was I a man after all?

I WANT A YA

Besides the usual academic pursuits school also made us proficient in book-binding, bee-keeping, sculpture, carpentry, baking, needle-point, Indian classical dance, Indian classical music, bag-pipe playing, tennis, horse riding, hockey, cricket, gymnastics and a host of other skills one could presumably use in daily life. What school was unable to provide us with, however, was some basic direction on how to deal with our raging hormones.

Because none of us had access to our parents for eight months of the year it was up to our teachers to deal with our development—mental, emotional and physical. The problem was that most of them appeared to be stuck in the Stone Age. They treated us like underage sex maniacs and so the way they dealt with our adolescence was to keep boys and girls as far away from one another as possible—a pointless exercise in a co-educational institution.

Every term, the student committee would organize a social and we all looked forward to it the way convicts look forward to conjugal visits. Deciding what to wear was a full-time job that began the preceding holiday. The week leading up to the social was one spent in empty-headed giddiness; we would spend hours each day figuring out the right accessories—this basically involved augmenting whatever we had managed to procure while at home by begging, borrowing and bullying it out of the other girls. The day of the dance itself was dedicated to hair and hair removal.

The night would commence with what was called the 'Grand Dinner', the grand part being that we got chicken and for many this was the highlight of the night. From there we moved on to Large Hall where all the action would go down. The Large Hall, where we usually assembled everyday before school, was converted into a dance hall, complete with talcum-powdered floors. This was a necessity because breakdancing was in, though with the exception of three students none of us were proficient, and so the powder allowed us to slide around as if we were doing the moonwalk. There was so much powder that the place smelled less like a club and more like a baby's nursery. Now that I think about it the floors looked like a bunch of cokeheads had been at it, but those were innocent times and I was oblivious of the existence of such things.

By the time we girls made it to the Large Hall the boys were already congregated there, milling about nervously while some cool kid's mix-tape played weakly from the sound system. I loved everything about the school dance though I have to say that whoever came up with the seating arrangement in the hall was a full-blown ass. The chairs were arranged against the walls so the girls and boys were placed around the dance floor, a good twenty-five feet away from each other and because of this foolishness once the dance started it took quite a few entreaties from the MC to get the boys to come over and ask us to dance. I didn't blame them. First, the guy had to screw up the courage to walk across this no-man's land to where the object of his affection was sitting, this had to be done with everyone and I mean everyone, watching. If she said 'yes I will dance with you' then he could stop sweating. If, on the other hand, she decided it was beneath her, which happened more often than one would think, he would have to slink back to his corner—with all of us giving his humiliation our full attention. Nonetheless, a few brave souls would get the ball rolling.

Dancing was the closest thing to sexual contact the school was willing to permit and to make sure nothing got out of hand we were chaperoned by several teachers, some of whom took their job way more seriously than the others. Naturally this added a level of tension that we didn't need; we were already bursting at the seams with dopamine. I can't speak for everyone but my goal was to try and make as much physical contact as possible with my crush. Luckily for me the committee came up with a few things to help people like me along. We were allowed a certain number of 'slow dances'—and even though this wasn't exactly salsa-type grinding it was still pretty good. But the best, and way more subversive moment we all waited for was the balloon dance. The balloon dance required you and your partner to balance a balloon between your foreheads. We couldn't look into each other's eyes but we were mere inches away from each other's mouths. I cannot imagine the boners this must have generated.

But this was about all the authorities could stand and so other than the social the general atmosphere around school was that contact of a romantic nature was wrong. If you had taken a good long look at most of our teachers this would not have surprised you. With the exception of our piano teacher Ms Elizabeth Thomas and our French teacher Mr Neelkanth Gupta, who ended up marrying each other, I was pretty sure none of the others even knew what romance was, forget actual sex. The idea of having a boyfriend or girlfriend wasn't even entertained by the staff and so, with no one to guide us when it came to the courting rituals of teenagers, like monkeys we simply imitated our seniors. While this was a sub-optimal solution it was the only one we had.

Our predecessors had put in place a system for when a boy wanted to ask a girl to be his babe. Basically, the boy in question would inform one of his friends of his desire, and this person would, in turn, carry the information to the lady. This process was called 'asking for a ya'. The 'ya' would be her saying yes to being his queen. Of course there was a pretty solid chance she would say 'no, thanks' and this was fine. In all likelihood the worst that would happen was his friends would make a lot of fun of him for a few days and then, if he had any gumption, he would move on to the next girl; if he didn't, he would live the rest of his life with the scars of rejection.

What irritated me then, as it does now, is that we girls had no such system. We had to wait, hoping like hell that the object of our affection would pick up on our heat and ask for a ya. I had wanted to ask for a ya on more occasions than I can count but I had to hold it in. We were not allowed to ask for a ya, our instructions included 'play hard to get', 'don't give it all away', and 'be mysterious'. I didn't understand any of this and still do not. I was dying to give it all away and didn't have the vaguest notion of what exactly I had to do to appear mysterious. As for playing hard to get, it was a concept I was unable to embody and so on the few occasions I was actually asked for a ya I had been so excited I had said ya immediately. Why wait? What for? What if he changes his bloody mind?

Varughese Thomas wants a ya. This news was brought to me by Mona D'Sa, my classmate and girlfriend of Rakesh Anthony aka BFF of Varughese. At the time of this proposal I was in the eighth grade, had no tits and wore braces; Varughese was in the ninth grade, sang songs as diverse as 'There's a Kind of Hush' and 'Eye of the Tiger', and had clearly not got a very good look at me. We had never spoken to each other. The fact that he wanted a ya from me came as a complete surprise and I said yes, please, before Mona had finished asking.

You don't even know him. This was Anuli, pointing out an obvious flaw in the relationship. Because she was doing nothing but acknowledging the facts, my response was characteristically immature. *Up yours,* I said and flounced off. Fuck her. I wasn't going to let her or anyone else rain on my parade. I now had a boyfriend. This was not some one-sided crush, it was legit.

Yes, we still hadn't spoken to one another but we had been exchanging glances during assembly and I was being properly teased by my classmates and his. Plus, it was easy for Anuli to have high standards, she was constantly being asked for a ya. As the best-looking girl in school, yas were being pelted at her daily. She had the luxury to say ya to someone she had actually had a conversation with. I did not.

Anyway, the point is that we did not have healthy role models on which to base any kind of sensible boy-girl interaction. Forget learning how to handle romance, it was clear we had no idea how to mingle at any level and by the time we got to the tenth grade the only way to describe the relationship we shared with our class boys was acrimonious—every day was war. After morning assembly at the Large Hall, where we were usually lectured to on the difference between good and evil, we would head over to our classrooms. As a girl, one never entered a classroom alone—we preferred to move in groups of three or more; and we never— ever—made eye contact with any of the boys. Accidental eye contact was usually greeted with *'Radhika Vaz! Fuck off'*.

It was perfectly normal to refer to someone by using their first, last, and middle name if it were available. This was because the use of just the first name sounded too polite and conveyed an air of warmth and tenderness. No matter how long the name we had to say it all. Sartaj Singh Gill, Rose Ann Shetty, Ajay Ratan Aggarwal, Anupama Katakam, or Tarun T. Kuruvilla—because we didn't know what the 'T' stood for, and so on.

Sometimes a whole hour would pass with me not having made eye contact. Having kept to one's self you would think that they would have left me alone but this was not the case.

'Radhika Vaz!' I would turn wearily knowing exactly what was coming my way.

It was usually either some variation involving the word 'fuck', the word 'bitch' or a line that one of the poet laureates from the backbench had come up with, such as *Vaz, shove it up your arse*. I actually liked this because at least it showed a modicum of creativity.

If the boys of my class were mini-savages, I wasn't much better. Instead of taking the high road and ignoring them, the way some of the other girls did, I tried to come up with stuff that would irritate them even more. My usual response to *Fuck off* and *Fuck you* was *You wish*. This would rile them further because it implied that they wanted to fuck me but that I was unwilling. I had learnt this from my dear friend Shefali Mahadik who was a batch ahead of me and who in my opinion was wise beyond her years. I used 'you wish' on a frequent basis and it never got old. It always elicited the exact level of frustration and anger I was aiming for.

Every now and then the boys would tire of the verbal back and forth and come up with new ways to torture us. One day I walked into class and discovered that my chair was missing. All the boys were clearly in on this one because when I asked Varkey Allapat and Premraj, who sat right behind me, if they had per chance seen my chair, they both said they hadn't even noticed it was missing and then made a big show of scanning the room to see if a spare chair was available. I decided that I would go get a chair from another classroom and just before leaving opened my desk to leave my satchel and books behind. There, inside my desk, was my chair—dismantled, Ikea style, by one of the carpentry wizards no doubt.

Much later, when I ran this story by my husband, his reaction was to pity my male classmates. Having studied in an all-boys boarding school himself he was unable to fathom the pain of seeing girls on a daily basis but not being allowed to touch or fidget with them.

I wouldn't have survived, he said shaking his head at the thought, *by the time I had to talk to girls I was in college and by then I had jerked off so much I was very calm.*

Clearly masturbation has its place.

MY VAGINA SPEAKS, DOES YOURS?

The first time my vagina farted I was in the ninth grade. I recall the moment with perfect clarity. It was library hour, my favourite time of the week, and the only time I felt like an adult. While we were still under the supervision of the librarian, Mr Selvaraj who, with a full grey beard and moustache, looked scary but actually wasn't, we weren't told what to do, and it was our time to do as we pleased. To begin with there was no homework that I had forgotten to do, no lesson that I hadn't been paying attention to, and no teacher who was sick of my sub-standard academic level and inability to 'apply myself'—an accusation I had to deal with on a daily basis. Basically, it was an hour to myself, or 'me-time', a concept I wasn't familiar with then but could still fully appreciate.

My more illustrious classmates would spend the hour reading a newspaper or studying for an exam, and the popular girls would spend their time being hit on by the popular boys. I would usually do one of three things: hang around the popular girls' periphery, take a nap or read literature I wasn't supposed to. The library was a private place and other than Mr Selvaraj there was no one else to spy on us doing anything untoward. Normally, this made no difference, our teachers were trained to catch us the moment we stepped out of line regardless of how outnumbered they were. What emboldened me to take the risks I did was the fact that Mr Selvaraj did not seem like any of the other teachers. He wasn't much of a disciplinarian, preferring instead to spend his time sorting through books, reading, or standing outside in the sun on days we had good weather. He was not, in other words, heavily invested in what happened to our brains while we were in his care—which was fine by me.

On the day in question I had smuggled in a Sidney Sheldon novel. I had a choice between studying *The Other Side of Midnight* and studying for an arithmetic test. Naturally, I chose smut. I had only recently become acquainted with Mr Sheldon and his fearless, horny heroines. There was one particular 'sex-scene', as we referred to them, which I was dying to read and I needed a safe space to read it, away from the prying eyes of my housemistress, and as far as I knew there was no place more secure than aisles U to Z. They were tucked away at the very far end of the library and I had spent many happy hours there. And so that is where I went to read about how Noelle Page made a mockery out of every single guy she fucked, although I was admittedly more interested in the fucking than I was in the mockery-making.

I was right at the part where Miss Page starts to blow the greasy, overweight proprietor of the shop she had just got a job at when I discovered that women have more than one orifice from which to expel air. A library is a rather unfortunate place to emit any bodily sound because no matter where in the world you may live the one thing a library is known for is its deafening silence and so my first reaction was to be grateful I was alone in my hiding place. My second was utter and complete confusion.

What just happened? I knew I had just passed wind but it most certainly had not taken the usual route. And then, it happened again. WTF! Was there perhaps something wrong with my plumbing? Was that meant to be a fart that just exited the wrong way? Was this biologically possible? Was this biologically necessary? Was this normal? Or—horror upon all horrors—was it just me? So many questions driven by so little air.

Until then I had no prior knowledge relating to such an

event. No one had ever told me about this, not my mum, not my teachers, not my friends, not even Sidney Sheldon—and he had told me about so much else. As far as I was concerned, in that moment, I was the only person with a talking vagina and I can assure you this was a heavy load to bear. I was mortified. My friends had already made it very clear to me that farting the normal way was a terribly unfeminine thing to do, only boys did it and if we did, we absolutely had to keep it to ourselves. There was absolutely no way they would understand this. If farting was a masculine activity then was I now twice the man I wasn't supposed to be? Even Sidney Sheldon's lewd sensibilities, that had until then held me captive, were incapable of consoling me and I made up my mind that this would be one of those things I would just keep to myself. I wouldn't even use it to get a laugh, a sacrifice I rarely made.

Naturally, I was on high alert for the next few days. A queef, unlike a regular fart, is hard to regulate. It is stealthy in build-up and swift upon exit, thus making it very hard to control. But when the phenomenon did not repeat itself, I just forgot all about it and carried on with my life. Over the next few years my punani did speak up from time to time, and while the shock had indeed worn off, the shame remained. I kept the entire business shrouded in secrecy in the belief that if no one else knew it meant that it had not actually happened.

As I got older I realized that concealment was virtually impossible. For one thing, my queefs are now less a girlish flutter and more a powerful vibration that feels like I have a motorboat engine tucked up my happy cavity causing a ten-fold increase in velocity at the time of release. I have also noticed that any inversion, headstands for example, are a definite instigator. These at least only take place during the practice of yoga which I now prefer to practice on my own. But the truly upsetting discovery came in my mid-twenties when, during a rather vigorous sexual encounter, I had the opportunity to learn that of all the storms that we women must weather, the timing of the pussy fart is most spectacular in its inappropriateness leaving me to explain to my paramour that 'that sound' was my intense orgasm.

Recently, my friend Kat told me about her grandma in Germany. Apparently, the woman queefs every time she stands up. All that this tells me is that women truly stop caring about what they look or sound like as they get older. And that, I suppose, is something to look forward to.

SCRAPED KNEES

By age fourteen I knew that athletes were the coolest people on earth. My father had presented me with *The Wills Book of Olympics* (a picture book on sports, fittingly sponsored by a cigarette company) that I was obsessed with. I knew as much as a knock-kneed girl deprived of athletic talent could possibly know about Jesse Owens, Valerie Briscoe Hooks, Emil Zatopeck, and Nadia Comaneci. Sure, I was unable to devote any time to conjugating French verbs or sorting out algebra but I knew all ten sporting events that made up the decathlon.

While I worshipped all these superhumans, I was partial to sprinters, and I was a major fan of both Florence Griffith Joyner and Edwin Moses. I wanted to be either one of them—muscular, graceful, fast and, above all else, world-famous. My new ambition coincided with the annual inter-house athletics competition and I decided that I would throw myself into preparing my body for it.

With nothing but air in my head I set about choosing an event. What would I dedicate myself to? It was obvious that I would need to pick something I had an actual chance of winning, and after mulling over the possibilities I had the nerve to settle on the 110-metre hurdle race. I was slightly taller than the average girl my age, and in my tiny mind this qualified me to compete in an event that, as far as I was concerned, involved jumping over several fence posts. While not as glamorous as winning the 100-metre dash Flo-Jo style, it was Edwin Moses' main event and so it would do.

I would like the reader to know that this was not my first athletic endeavour. I was a proud member of the school hockey team (granted I was on it mostly for my ability to get along well with everyone) and I considered myself to be in peak physical shape. It was with this optimistic frame of mind that I approached my first training day.

It was a standard mid-April morning up in the Nilgiri Hills—clear, crisp and sunny. The athletics ground was called Top Flats, a huge field with bleachers on two sides for spectators. I made my way to Top Flats in the company of Anita—the best athlete in my age group and possibly the entire school. The girl did not run, she flew, and was part of a group of students whose athletics training was overseen by Mr Boppiah and Mr Bharathan—our coaches. I was not part of this elite group but Anita happened to be going to Top Flats a little early to warm-up and so I would be able to pretend we were peers. Just walking with her was inspiring, and by the time I got there I knew that today was the day that the Lawrence School would be introduced to yet another sportsperson of note.

With Anita by my side it did not occur to me that one day of preparation would be supremely inadequate. Instead, my mind was filled with the screams of all the fans as they saw me, the wild card, defeat the other competitors. Who knew, maybe the 100-metre dash—the holiest of holy grails—was next.

The warm-up felt more like an all-out sprint to me but I hung in there. The hurdles had already been set up in anticipation of the first round of heats which were to be held the following afternoon so Anita suggested we do a quick warm-up run down the 110 metre hurdle track. Anita went first and as I collected myself and my breath I watched her carefully because I knew I would need to replicate everything she did. She crouched at the starting line (the way sprinters do) and then she was off—soaring over each hurdle in perfect form. She finished and jogged back to me.

Now it was my turn. I could hear the fans going nuts in the bleachers—but I would tune them out. I needed to focus. I simulated Anita's starting crouch.

GO! yelled Anita and I did.

As I charged towards the first hurdle I saw myself, gazelle-like, leaping into the air, effortlessly clearing one obstacle after another. With the theme song from *Flashdance* ('What a Feeling' by Irene Cara) playing in my head, I sailed over the first hurdle and the next thing I knew I was face-down in a cloud of dust wishing I were dead.

Oh my God, Radhika, are you okay?!

Blood was gushing from a deep gash on my knee but I didn't even notice, busy as I was contemplating the fact that my athletic career was not to be. On seeing my knee Anita suggested we go to the hospital. She even offered to come with me but it was too late because the rest of the actual athletes were beginning to gather and she would have to join them. I had no intention of going to the hospital. I knew I would get a tetanus injection and there was no way that was happening; of all the things that I am afraid of, needles are high on the list; it is possibly the only thing that stands between me and heroin addiction. So, I limped back to the dorms, washed my injury, stuck a band-aid on it and went about my life.

A few days later the cut was properly infected and the following Sunday I nervously made my way to the hospital. My knee hurt and I knew a tetanus injection was a sure thing. As I entered the first-aid room my misery immediately gave way to fear because there seated behind the desk and reading her morning newspaper was the Duty Nurse—Sister Megan Ricketts.

The school hospital was Sister Megan's fiefdom; she ruled the roost and no one (not even the doctor) dared cross her. She was always dressed in a spotless white calf-length dress, white cardigan, white stockings, white flat shoes and, sitting on her head like a little crown, was her white nurse's hat. And while she certainly was a large woman she didn't look fat; she looked strong—like all her weight was muscular. Her pink cheeks and light eyes had once, very long ago, misled me into believing she was a kind Florence Nightingale-type person whose only joy was found in making people feel better. I was wrong.

My last experience with Sister Megan was from three years ago. I was sent to the hospital because I had the flu. I was housed with five other sickos in the girls' ward. Dinner was served promptly at seven and consisted of rice kanji, a gruel that defies description, and a cup of milk. A firm believer that no food should ever be wasted no matter how disgusting it was, Sister Megan usually stuck around to watch us eat. That evening however her attention was required elsewhere. I hated milk and so the moment she left the room I decided that I would dispose of it.

Stealth and swiftness were of the essence. I grabbed my mug and rushed to the bathroom where I hurriedly emptied the contents into the sink all the while congratulating myself on having pulled this off despite my ward-mates' advice against it. Smiling smugly to myself I whipped around and almost bumped right in to Sister Megan. She had sneaked up on me in those soft-soled nurses' shoes. I thought I was going to faint.

RADHIKA VAZ! What do you think you are doing?

All 200 pounds of Sister Megan bawled at me.

In the dining room, now!

I ran back into the dining room with Sister Megan in pursuit. I was shitting myself by now. I knew she was old-school and a big believer in corporal punishment. Plus, it was clear that she wanted to make an example out of me. The other patients all sat there white-faced as she yelled at all of us.

Do you think this is a joke? she screamed—her face and both chins a disturbing shade of crimson.

Do you think throwing away your milk is funny? How do you

expect to get better? No, you don't want to get better, you want to sit here sick and weak—that is all you children are good for.

She then picked a sturdy wooden spatula off the table and proceeded to give the palms of my dainty little hands a sound walloping.

Ever since then, whenever Sister Megan saw my parents, she would let them know in no uncertain terms that they should not have spared the rod, that I was a smart mouth without any of the required smarts, and that one day I would get my comeuppance. Clearly that day had come. I was completely at her mercy and I was sure she was going to kill me. Now that I have lived a little I realize two things. Working on a Sunday stinks and seeing a client that you think is a worthless oaf on that Sunday stinks even harder.

Radhika Vaz! What are you doing here? she thundered.

I fell on Top Flats and cut my knee, I quivered.

On uncovering what was now a disgusting, septic-looking wound Sister Megan's eyes almost popped out of her head and I knew I was in big trouble.

When did this happen?

A few days ago. I mumbled vaguely.

WHEN, EXACTLY?

Last week, I said, trembling like a leaf.

What idiot sits quietly with this for one week? This is terrible— you might need stitches!

I started to cry immediately.

Please, Sister! Please don't give me stitches. Anything except stitches.

My wailing and Sister Megan's normal speaking voice brought Sister Annapurna to the first-aid room.

So loudly this girl is crying! What happened? Someone died or what?

Sister Annapurna was second in command and the physical opposite of Sister Megan. She was tall, thin, dark-skinned and always wrapped in a pristine white sari. But other than that they were two peas in a pod, bonded together in their common distaste of bratty, sick kids. My nightmare was getting worse.

This fool has gone and fallen. LAST WEEK. Somewhere-or-the-other doing God-only-knows-what. It's infected and now she comes crying 'Oh Sister, please help me'.

Though they spent the next few minutes debating the need for stitches, they were in complete agreement on my incredible stupidity, and the fact that they were both having such a nice, quiet morning until now. They finally decided it was too late for stitches, and that I would require a tetanus injection. But before any of that they would have to clean up my knee which was now a cesspool and was definitely going to hurt like hell.

With anyone else I would have wept and wailed but with Sister Megan I sat there without making a sound, one hand clenching the bed and the other one wrapped around Sister Annapurna's boney arm. Knowing full well what would happen to me if I cried or made a fuss Sister Annapurna tried to distract me. We chatted mainly about boys and my sad-sack love life seemed to amuse both nurses greatly. Because I am easily encouraged by laughter I started to think that these two women were my new BFFs and I was about to start on a new story when Sister Megan announced that she was done with my knee and wanted to get some tea, so would Sister Annapurna please administer the injection.

Besides being crushed that she wasn't into my story, I was horrified that I would not have anyone to cling to in my darkest hour. It was probably the look of desperation on my face that kept her there and as Sister Annapurna got ready to skewer me, Sister Megan held my hand—the very same one she had battered three years ago.

SUDDEN DEATH

The thing with boarding school is that you never consider life after it. Not being exposed to anything other than the school campus for eight months of the year means that your world really is a very small bubble. I loved my bubble and what I did not know was that this bubble was about to burst. Here is how it happened.

I had just finished my tenth grade final exam and was enjoying my summer holidays at home. I was hoping I had done well enough to be re-admitted for the last two years of school. Actually, I wasn't hoping anything, I had taken for granted that I would be going back because, like I said, it was my bubble and I didn't know anything existed outside of it. Per regular procedure, we were all notified via mail of our acceptance back to school shortly after our grades were released, and while mine weren't great I was well aware they were not the worst either. So I waited for what would surely be a formality.

Then it arrived. The envelope was addressed to my dad but as it was decorated with the school insignia I opened it myself with the intention of showing it to my parents later that day. I do not recall exactly how the epistle was worded but in essence its purpose was to inform my parents that I, in the estimation of the entire teaching staff, was badly behaved, of inferior intellect, had a boy crazy, disruptive streak, and hence would not be welcome back to complete high school. It politely asked that my parents begin making alternative arrangements for my further education.

It was signed by the school headmaster.

I was so stunned that if someone had stuck a knife in me I probably wouldn't have felt a thing. Okay, well, maybe not a knife but a needle—which is saying a lot. I had to read that note several times, first because I could not believe it and then because I thought by reading it multiple times I might be able to change what it had to say. How could this be happening? That place was my home. I knew everyone. My classmates, my seniors whose behinds I kissed, my juniors who kissed mine, Joe and Nagaraj, our dining hall bearers, who gave me extra food, Harriet and Umni, in the kit room, who let me off the hook when I lost part of my kit, looking the other way on numerous occasions so that my parents wouldn't get a bill for lost pillow covers. I knew these people better than I knew my own mum and dad and now I wouldn't see them again. Possibly ever. What was going to happen to me? I felt like my family had suddenly been obliterated.

Of course when you compare my plight to that of children in war-torn countries it is very hard to sympathize but at that time I was pretty sure that no one had it as bad as I did. My shock eventually gave way to panic. Not being allowed back to school was a sharp enough kick to the proverbial nuts but to be told that I couldn't go back because I was always in trouble, not too bright and horny—that was a KO à la Mike Tyson. I was too freaked out to even cry because I was busy being petrified of my parents' reaction to this news. Thus far I had seen other friends' parents react really badly to news of a similar nature, including a girl whose dad had slapped her when he heard she had a boyfriend. If one lousy boyfriend could turn her own family against her then what was to become of me? I remember reading about students who committed suicide because they had disappointed their families. I had never been able to understand what drove them to this extreme level of shame. Now I did.

There was no way I could physically hand this letter over to my dad and so I folded it, re-glued the envelope and left it with the rest of the mail. By nightfall I knew that he had to have seen the letter so I kept out of everyone's way the best I could. Finally my parents cornered me. They calmly explained that I would probably not be going back to school and then my dad asked,

Have you been in any trouble recently? Anything out of the ordinary, I mean.

I wracked my brain for anything that stood out from my usual shenanigans. Now, I hadn't exactly been a model student but these accusations were way off base and I knew for a fact that there was no way the authorities could have known about my first kiss in the new junior school building. Or the second one in the headmaster's own home for that matter.

There was, however, one other incident. A few months before the term had ended one of my very best friends had been busted for smoking and had been expelled good and proper. She was the first girl who told me she knew exactly what a penis looked like because she had seen one—more than a friend I was her fan and had accompanied her on several of her smoke breaks, usually behind the school church (not very original) and sometimes to the grass pitch. Someone had obviously snitched on her, to this day we don't know who, including informing the authorities where she kept her ciggies.

Because she and I were thick I was called in for questioning. They obviously didn't need to ask me anything because they had confiscated everything including her cigarettes but not knowing any of this I did what I have been trained to do—I was her friend and so I lied in her defence. All the teachers in attendance had called me a liar for indeed that is what I was. I told my parents this whole story because I was sure it would come out sooner or later and, I am embarrassed to admit this, I hoped that they would view my own misdemeanours more leniently when they heard of this other much more serious infraction.

My parents took all this in and then my dad turned to my mother. *This guy is a fucking idiot,* he said, referring to my headmaster, *he needs his arse kicked.* This was not said with anger or bitterness but with a matter-of-factness, immediately after which he launched into what can only be described as a paper-based fight to the death with the school's headmaster as his unsuspecting opponent.

You know when people say 'enjoy the process, don't worry about the end result'—well my pops took that to a whole new level, revelling in every moment of it. He was delighted with how well he constructed his nasty letters and he pulled the whole 'just because I am an air force officer and not an important person, poor us' card with flair. He didn't stop at clichés either, he found a list of all the kids with lower grades than mine who had somehow made it back to school and shoved that down the headmaster's gullet, he dedicated page upon page to reaming out the archaic policies the school had around boy–girl relations, and he asked the most important question of all: If indeed I was such a shitty kid why was he being informed of this so late? Why indeed.

His intention was to expose the headmaster as a man who promoted ass-kissing and favouritism and thus cause him some measure of humiliation in front of the school's Board of Directors. Once he had finished doing that he decided to go the extra mile and kept up the harassment until he had the headmaster wishing my dad and I were both dead and offering for me to come back to school. By this time though I didn't really want to go back. It was all too much for my fifteen-year-old heart. I didn't think I could face everyone, and I knew that life wouldn't be too much fun given that my dad had indeed succeeded in making the headmaster look like a complete tool, and so I changed schools, yet again.

The only good that came of all this was that I was now pretty clear who my family really was. And while they were still pretty weird they were getting a little less so.

I FIND A NEW GROUP OF FRIENDS, AND PORN

With great difficulty my parents managed to enrol me into Mount Carmel College, Bangalore. It was an all-girls college, a good thing, given my easily distracted nature. Because I had spent the whole summer thinking I was going back to school I had not bothered to make friends with the girls who lived on my street, but my mum, bless her heart, had taken the trouble to do just that and had found out that Brenda D'Souza, who lived four houses down, was enrolled at the same place. And so, on the first day of college, I actually had company.

Brenda and I became close friends over the next few months but on that first day, and as soon as her brother dropped us off at the main gate, she was swallowed up by a heaving mass of girls from her high school who had all joined Mount's (as it was affectionately, and in my opinion inappropriately, called for short). I did not have this luxury so I did my best to keep Brenda in my line of vision and followed the entire group of excited women into the college auditorium where we were to be given an orientation programme of sorts. In there, I was reunited with Brenda, after she noticed me lurking on the periphery, and she then introduced me to Gayathri who, like me, was enrolled in the liberal arts programme. I decided I wasn't going to let Gayathri out of my sight.

Turns out she had more or less the same idea. Colleges in India are well known for one thing—hazing, a ritual that all newbies are put through and it ranges from harmless fun to misadventures that end up making newspaper headlines, which is why we rubes believed that there was safety in numbers. Gayathri and I clung to each other that first week. At Mount's (why do I keep thinking of dogs having sex?) the hazing amounted to harmless fun designed more to embarrass than to hurt. They would make us sing and dance while they laughed their asses off at our shame. I did a pretty good job of pretending I felt uncomfortable with their requests but in my head I was going 'what a fucking joke'—this was what I lived for, making people laugh and here I had to do nothing but sing and dance badly and they were rolling around on the floor. My enthusiasm may have dampened their fun a little and very soon we were being left alone to continue on our journey of learning.

As the weeks went by Gayathri and I developed a kinship that went beyond needing protection. A month into our classes and we absorbed Sonali Roy (who I will always refer to by using both first and last name). Then, in French class we met Anandi (aka Andy). Then one day at lunch I was introduced to a real bigmouth called Kalpana (like forces sometimes attract), then I was invited to a birthday party where I met Ruch and, gradually, as it goes with sixteen-year-olds, a posse began to form. The pain of my untimely ejection from Lovedale was still a little raw but time was doing its thing and I was finding new friends. I was still a little insecure though as most of these girls, being local Bangaloreans, had known each other since they were kids. So I didn't realize how very much a part of this group I was until the event of Kalpana's sixteenth birthday. To celebrate this joyous occasion we had decided that we would, in addition to the picnic lunch that had been planned, congregate at Gayathri's place and watch a porno.

Having grown up without the Internet, it turned out their exposure to porn was as limited as mine. Until then all I had seen were several issues of *Debonair*—the Indian answer to *Playboy*. I was nine and my friend Ira's dad was heavily into *Debonair*; he had many issues of the magazine hidden in a box on top of a cupboard in his study and, luckily for us, Ira's brother had managed to find this stash. And so, one day when the parents were out, our little group of pre-teens got together and reviewed every issue we could lay our hands on. We spent several hours giggling at pictures of women's breasts and what little we thought we could see through their panties. As far as I recall there were no crotch shots but there was plenty of boobage and ass-cleavage to go around. *Debonair* also had a bunch of really sexy stories about sluts who didn't care if you were married and would have wild sex with you. Based on this recollection I figured that watching a moving picture version of such a story would be even more titillating.

Procuring the film turned out to be a bit of a chore. Andy's brother was a member of the Vasant Nagar video library and he assured us that despite its 'family friendly' appearance it would have what we needed. The ten of us made our way to the video place and on our way it was decided that Andy would ask for the product. She would be assisted by Neepa, who was selected based on the fact that she was a year ahead of us and would bring much needed gravitas to the proceedings. The rest of us would wait at the far end of the store.

We then paraded in rather confidently but our swagger evaporated as soon as we realized there wasn't one but three shop assistants, all young guys probably in their mid-twenties. Clearly they were having a very slow day and so when we barged in they all came over to offer their assistance. The chattiest of the three volunteered to help us.

Yes, madam, he smirked at Andy, clearly recognizing her from the last time she had innocently rented *Back to The Future*. We watched in pain as Andy and Neepa hemmed and hawed and finally screwed up the courage to throw down our opening gambit.

Do you have any triple-X rated films?

This is what we had come up with earlier; we were either going big or going home. Triple-X and nothing less. We wanted to see some cock for heaven's sake, in as many shapes, sizes and colours as we possibly could.

Madam, we don't have triple-X only double-X, he informed them thus dealing our strategy a body blow.

I see, said Neepa very calmly, and then the two scuttled back to us with this news. We huddled together to discuss this setback.

Will this double-X nonsense have a penis in it?

How do I know?

Your brother rents his videos here, you should have asked him.

Why don't you ask your brother then?

I don't have a brother.

We were getting nowhere and were acutely aware of the undivided attention we were getting from the three salesmen. Realizing that beggars can't be choosers we sent Anandi, this time backed by both Neepa and Kalpana (it was her bloody birthday after all), to request the gentlemen to please suggest a title. After a short discussion, the details of which we were not privy to, one of the sales guys disappeared into the back room and reappeared with a film titled *Pink Ladies*.

It turns out that one should be very specific about what it is one wants to see because what we found ourselves saddled with was two hours of girl-on-girl sex. A man did make an appearance at the very end but it was a cameo of sorts; he played the creep who gets caught jerking off while watching a group of young women take a shower and we barely glimpsed his knob.

This is stupid, Gayathri declared, although she did appear mildly flushed.

I hope those guys aren't jerking off thinking of us watching this movie, said Anjali, always concerned about what other people were thinking.

Disgusting! I proclaimed as I continued to watch one lady

give head to three others in quick succession. What made this scene so compelling was that the three recipients of the woman's favour were all playing musical instruments during the act. I am absolutely sure that every single one of us went home and wanked ourselves into a trance but we all declared that in general what we had just viewed was despicable.

The following year—yes, we absolutely had to do this in yearly cycles—on Kalpana's seventeenth birthday we circumvented video libraries and asked Sonali Roy's boyfriend to get us something.

Make sure it has a man's dick in it, I instructed her when she made the call.

What we got was a film with the promising title of *Pleasure Hunt Part 1*. We hoped for the best and it was, an all-out hetero hump fest with money shots of the male organ from every conceivable angle. We all watched silently, thoroughly engrossed until the credits rolled, and once again none of us admitted to being remotely turned on by any of it. In fact, some of us went as far as to claim we felt ill from watching some of the procedures being performed.

Later the same night Ruch and I started talking.

I didn't know a blow job involved almost choking to death, I said.

Not really choking, just gagging, said Ruch, ever the voice of reason, as I would come to find out.

That's true, I agreed, *I guess it wasn't that bad.*

No, it wasn't, she concurred, and then in a leap of faith she lowered her voice and whispered to me, *actually I was pretty turned on.*

Me too! I was so relieved to have this weight off my chest.

Let's not tell anyone else, though.

Yes, let's not.

And with that I knew I was home. I had shared a secret and was in possession of someone else's. Life was good.

IF THIS IS VIRGINITY, YOU CAN HAVE MINE

'Like a virgin, touched for the very first time.'
—Madonna, 1985

To anyone who was around in the 80s these words aren't just familiar, they were an anthem. Like every other tween at the time, I adored Madonna and could be found standing in front of the mirror happily belting out the lyrics despite the fact that I had no idea what the word virgin even meant. A few years later, in senior school, I had read just enough smut to be intellectually aware of what virginity was, but it would be a few years more before I became aware of its importance in society—especially if one were a girl.

While in boarding school, though, I didn't think about it at all. As far as I knew, we were all virgins, which is why I didn't view my own, or anyone else's, virginity as special. We were simply people who had not had sex because we weren't supposed to, the same way we weren't supposed to smoke cigarettes or drink alcohol. It was one of those things that just was—I had eyes, ears, kidneys and this hymen gizmo. I am aware I was raised in more innocent times, there was no Internet or social media and so there was considerably less peer pressure than there is now. And never mind sex, my generation grew up thinking kissing was a big deal.

My own first kiss was conducted in the stairwell of the new junior school building—a location chosen in collaboration with my best friend Dia. We decided it would be the perfect venue because it was still partially under construction and hence completely deserted on weekends. It was also cold and brightly lit but that did not matter. I was less interested in ambience and more concerned with keeping this operation as covert as possible. The more I think about it the more the whole operation resembled a bank robbery. We had three people whose job it was to KV or 'keep vigilance' in case anyone, student or staff, got uncomfortably close to the scene. We also had an exit strategy if we had to abandon our efforts abruptly. I would run up the stairs with Dia and leave from the front of the building while the boy and his two cronies would split by running down the hill at the back.

While our security detail would have put a mid-level rapper's entourage to shame, the real reason they were there wasn't so much that they would prevent anything from going down, although we hoped they would, but that if something *did* happen then at least there were five of us in the building—and unless the authorities accused us of conducting an orgy it would be hard to sell the idea that anything else was going on. Basically, our friends were putting their own necks on the line so we could get our rocks off but that is boarding school friendship for you. As a final precaution I kept my mouth firmly closed the whole time. If I got caught kissing a boy I wanted, with a clean conscience, to tell everyone I didn't allow any tongue.

Afterwards, I spent several days thinking about the kiss. Of course, I had enjoyed it but it didn't change anything. I was the same, my boyfriend was the same, and Ms Shreedhar was still boring me to death in Math class. While the act itself had been exciting, the aftermath was unremarkable. It wasn't that I was instantly jaded, but just a little surprised that, with all the hoopla and tension that surrounds any kind of physical contact between boys and girls, things go back to exactly as they always had been.

If nothing changes then why was everyone in our business trying to control our every move? Given the kind of stress involved in organizing a safe environment wherein one can conduct some pretty basic smooching, it was unlikely that any of us were going to try and attempt anything that required the time-consuming act of taking off and putting on clothing. Perhaps that was their plan.

Once I left boarding school and headed to Bangalore, however, I started to look at things a little differently. I was sixteen, in a day school, and with limited adult supervision that left me free to do as I pleased between the hours of 8 a.m. and 4 p.m. I had friends who had friends who were making the most of their freedom. Now, all of a sudden, being a virgin or not being one was an actual choice we could exercise and that is all we talked about.

Do you think Anu is a virgin? We were talking about a student in her final year of college and five years our senior. Anu's boyfriend was a working guy who was even older than her and he had a beard, which is what made me wonder about them. I was and still am of the belief that older guys with beards are definitely not interested in dating virgins. Plus, she smoked cigarettes, another definite sign of an active sex life.

No, she's not. This was Shalini who despite being our year was friendly with all the seniors and my window into their world. *But she and Vincent have been going around for three years and they are getting married.*

All of us had bought into the idea that if you were planning on getting married to the guy then losing your virginity to him was perfectly acceptable. If, however, you just wanted to have sex and had no future plans with the gentleman involved then you were a slut—and as a slut you would never find anyone decent to marry. In fact, it wasn't just us who believed this, the entire country believed it—and needless to say, we still hold virgins in very high regard. I made this discovery one day while reading the *Deccan Herald*. Back then single people didn't have Tinder and

Grinder and all the online luxuries you have today. Instead they advertised for a spouse in the newspaper, in a special segment called the 'Personals', and this along with the funnies was the only part of the news I was interested in.

The personals, despite being so public, made me feel like I was being told a secret. It fascinated me that a Saraswat Brahmin man's parents had taken the trouble to write up a little sales pitch for their son seeking what seemed like the female version of him. Of course, by the late-80s, 'caste no bar' was trending and many families were finally opening up to the fact that it was okay to let their children mingle a little. But while one's caste was becoming slightly less of an issue, one's virginity remained a major selling point. I learnt this one morning when I came across a description of a woman who, among other things, was an 'innocent divorcee'.

Dad, what's an innocent divorcee?
A divorced person who didn't consummate the marriage.
What's consummate?
Please go speak to your mother.

Aha! So that was what an innocent divorcee was. And now she and her intact hymen were seeking a second chance that I for one fully believed she deserved. I always wondered who helped her write that ad. And, more importantly, who was the shrewd cookie who, recognizing her innocence as her most valuable asset, made it the opening act of the piece, thus pushing her fair skin and Green Card to second and third fiddle respectively. With all that I know today I am going to assume it was her pops, because as a man he must have known that no other man would want to marry a dirty little whore.

Based on everything I had gleaned it was clear that virginity was at a premium. It was like a beautiful jewel we had been given to take care of and there was just one thing we had to keep in mind—we couldn't hand it over to just anyone. Our first time absolutely had to be special. And because defining what's special and what isn't would be too tedious, not to mention meaningless, the same people who decided that female virginity was sacred also concluded that giving it up to the husband within the blessed bonds of matrimony was the safest way to go. Why tax a young woman's mind with trying to figure out the specialness quotient of a man? Instead, use a blanket rule: fuck only your husband or you will go to hell. Having been repeatedly hit over the head with the message that my virginity would greatly increase my worth as a woman, I actually believed that one day I too would present my husband with the gift of an unused vagina.

I did not question the idiocy of this sentiment but at some point however I did question whether or not an unused penis held quite the same allure. I was quickly dispelled of any such notion. Unlike women, a virgin man is a joke, a sap who has no game whatsoever. While women the world over are having their hymens surgically resealed to maintain their 'virginity', men are expected to do everything in their power to lose theirs. How these two inherently antithetical expectations were simultaneously possible was the biggest puzzle.

None of this made any sense whatsoever and, with each passing day, I became more and more convinced that this whole virginity thing was overrated rubbish. What was the big deal about losing it? For one thing, it wasn't even a particularly useful, or visible, body part, like a foot. If I lost my foot everyone would notice and I wouldn't be able to wear Nike high-tops. If I lost my virginity, on the other hand, nobody would notice and I could continue to wear Nike high-tops. My virginity brought nothing to the party, it just sat there doing bugger all. Yet losing it was going to be a very, very big deal. As if it were something you could actually lose in the first place. *Oh no, I just lost my virginity. How careless of me! It's the second time this week!*

My resolve was fading fast. I was sixteen, for crying out loud, and at this point in my life marriage seemed as distant a concept as death. Sure, we had all been told to wait, that it would be worth it, and what not, but now I was really beginning to wonder—how much longer was I to guard my precious punani? And what if I never got married! What provisions if any had been made for that eventuality? NOTHING! These people who were sitting wherever making up the rules had obviously thought none of this through. Maybe this had worked out for the generation of women before us but I wasn't impressed and quite frankly by this time I knew, deep down in my soul, that I would not be holding out for a wedding ring. Not because I didn't want to but because I knew I couldn't. I was horny, curious and, above all else, human.

I was also scared. The problem with all the pro-virginity propaganda that one is bludgeoned with on a daily basis is that it frightens you. Besides thinking that I would immediately die of AIDS or a botched abortion there was the moral aspect to contend with—a point brought home to me as I was busy figuring out where I would go to college. I was particularly keen on moving to Bombay. It sounded like a fun thing to do and I wouldn't be alone, my dad's family all live around there.

Unlike most extended families, ours usually tended to keep their opinions to themselves, but on the issue of my higher learning they were surprisingly vocal. My cousin Sandy was beside himself with worry. He is the eldest of all us cousins, and considered himself worldly, having been raised in Bombay. As far as he was concerned, we were just small town folk who knew nothing.

Aunty Surya, he said to my mum, *let me just tell you one thing. Just one thing—Sophia College chicks have the worst reputation, they are all fast chicks and if she goes there she will become fast as well.*

'Fast chicks' are girls who put out left and right without giving a shit about what anyone has to say. Of course, Sandy's point of view did not surprise anyone—certain women's colleges in India enjoy a less than saintly reputation amongst the male population.

And while it is entirely possible that the behaviour of some students may have compromised the standing of these venerable institutions, I was pretty sure that more men had been turned down than turned on by these so-called sluts. Yet, my cousin was afraid that mere contact with these women would immediately turn me into one. How? Was sluttery contagious? And were all the sluts being quarantined in women's-only colleges? Frankly, these women sounded like fun but I kept that to myself, there was far too much judgment floating in the air and I didn't want to catch any of it.

As I rolled my eyes I caught sight of Uncle Yves (RIP) who sat there with a look on his face that said he too thought my cousin was talking out of his rear end. It turned out that he was far less concerned about the college turning me into a slut. He suspected something far more diabolical that that. *You know, Surya, if you send her to that place they'll turn her into a nun. That is exactly what they do.*

These were the alternatives, I could choose between being a big fat slore or a big fat virgin. There was no discussion of me becoming an economist or a teacher—or a comedian for that matter. Nope—my only options were to become a woman of loose morals or a woman trying to enforce stricter ones. And this is why young women in India never talk to their families about anything. I, for one, knew exactly which way I was going to swing my virginity vote.

I was torn (no pun intended) and I needed help. Before I whoopsie-daisy lost my virginity I needed for my girl friends to tell me it was okay, the same way they had said that my acid wash jeans and bolo ties were okay. But I had to be very careful about who to go to.

Anu. Would you have sex before marriage? I knew she wasn't going to come out and tell me she was already humping the Beard—she and I weren't that kind of close—but I expected honesty and I got it. *Only if I really loved the guy*, she said, as she puffed on an illicit Gold Flake.

LOVE! There was the loophole I had been looking for. According to Anu, if I fell in love, and who was to say I hadn't, then I could shag with wild abandon, or at least with abandon. Marriage was the Holy Grail, of course, but Love, according to Anu, had the ability to sanitize the dirtiness of pre-marital sex. If you loved then you weren't a slut, you were in fact like a virgin being touched for the very first time. I was greatly relieved by this philosophy although it would be a few more years before I was able to put it all to practical use.

BEAUTY SCOUT

It was the 90s, Madhu Sapre had lost the Miss Universe title by a hair's breadth, but in a watershed moment the following year, Sushmita Sen and Aishwarya Rai won Miss Universe and Miss World and I went quietly mad with glee. Finally, the world had realized how beautiful we Indian women truly were. This was my moment and I was going to carpe diem the shit out of it. Of course, I didn't have a plan or a modelling portfolio; I was too cool and good-looking for that. Instead, I decided that the best way to get my career rolling was to be 'spotted' by a model coordinator as I went about my daily business. There were a surprising number of them floating about Bombay spotting models all day long. I merely had to wait.

By the time I got to my third, and final, year of college I was more than a little concerned. My charisma and good looks had remained undiscovered. I was almost twenty, an economics major in striking distance of flunking every single course I was enrolled in, and with no real understanding of economics except that I needed money to lead a happy and fulfilling life. Money that I did not have and, quite frankly, had no clue how to get. With less than six months left to graduate I needed a plan. Well, actually I needed a miracle. And then it happened.

My friend Sneha's brother got married and invited Sneha's closest friends to his very fancy pre-wedding party. By fancy what I mean is 'grown-up'. He and his friends were proper adults; they were in their late twenties and had jobs. I wasn't into older guys or anything but I knew that this wasn't the same as a college party and my immediate concern was with regard to wardrobe and make-up. I had the worst clothes and owned no make-up and so I spent the week preceding the party running around borrowing stuff to put an outfit together.

On the night of the party we rolled in eight deep, me and my then posse, thinking we were so cool. I was dressed to kill in my friend Anandi's party jeans, Gayatri's sleeveless black t-shirt, and Smita's black brogues. The party was the best I had ever been to until then, there was catered food, a bar with a bartender who treated me like a paying customer, a DJ who played every single song I requested. And, if that wasn't enough, the venue was a rooftop, which was ideal; there was loads of space to show off my moves. Moves I had gleaned over the years from *Flashdance*, *Footloose*, and *Dirty Dancing*. Those were truly the days of dancing like nobody was watching us.

About a week later I was busy cutting an Econometrics lecture so I could take a much needed nap when, in the distance, I heard the hall phone ringing in its usual annoying high pitch.

Vaz! It's for you.

Goddamn it. A phone call for me? My then-boyfriend lived in another city and only called on the weekends, and my parents never called. Who the hell was calling on a Wednesday afternoon—it was nap time.

Hello?

Is that Radhika? a self-assured, female voice inquired.

Yes.

Radhika, my name is Deepa. I met you at Jai's party last week.

I remembered her—she had told me I had personality. I recall being slightly annoyed by the comment because I had been hoping my looks would do the talking that night.

Anyway, I work for Anaita Advani.

ANAITA ADVANI! She was, at the time, the best-known

model scout. My heart was thumping and I warmed to Deepa immediately.

And we are in the middle of casting the Limca ad.

LIMCA AD! Limca was one of the biggest soft drink brands and my personal favourite vodka mixer. I had thrown up vodka and Limca many times and to this day I remember everything about their iconic TV ads from the 90s. Limca cast only the prettiest young thing AND she became instantly famous. This was a role I would blow out of the water. Thank god I'd worn Anandi's jeans and not my own rubbish; I had had a sixth sense about the party all along!

Are you still there, Radhika?

Yes, still here.

We are wondering, would you be interested in coming in for a screen test.

INTERESTED! Of course I was interested, this was the moment I had been holding my goddamn breath for. Three fucking years of sitting through boring lectures and suffering the nuns who ran the hostel I lived in was finally paying off—I was being discovered! I would be the next Mehr Jessia, the next Madhu Sapre…screw India—I would be the next Linda Evangelista. I could already see my 5'6" frame nonchalantly parading up and down the catwalks of London, Milan and Paris. My life was falling into place. I would never have to attend another Statistics class, I could forget everything I knew about game theory, I was being rescued.

Hello Radhika?

I'm here, I gasped.

Okay good. So this is the best number to reach you at?

It was actually the only number to reach me at, *YES, this is the number!*

Good, so someone will be in touch in the next few days.

Okay—well, bye then.

Bye.

I hung up making a mental note to stay mum about the whole business of my future fame until the screen test was done. For one, I did not want to jinx it and, for another, I didn't want any of my friends to feel bad that they had not been picked. And why hadn't they been picked? They were definitely all prettier than I was…or were they? I was secretly pleased they hadn't been called; victory would be so much sweeter now that I didn't need to share it. And so with these selfish thoughts I floated back to my room to admire my face that was fast becoming my fortune.

I won't lie, the first twenty-four hours were hard—like a junkie on her way down, I was distracted and jumpy. What would I wear to the screen test? What would they make me do at this screen test? Would I have to dance and sing the jingle, or were they already so enamoured with my beauty and personality that this was all a mere formality?

The next twenty-four hours were worse. I had moved from anxiety-ridden addict to desperate lover. I woke up with Deepa's name in my head; why hadn't Deepa called, had she changed her mind, had she found someone better looking, had she lost my number? What if she had tried calling and missed me! Our stupid community phone did not have an operator, so that was entirely possible. Perhaps I should just stop going to class altogether and stay by the phone; perhaps I should ask Sneha to call her brother so we could track Deepa down. No—that was pathetic and certainly something Linda Evangelista would never do.

Three days later it was clear to me what was going on. I was going to have to pass my final-year exams, I was going to have to tolerate the nuns and their draconian rules, I was going to have to get a job. I was not going to be snatched from the jaws of real life with a lucrative modelling contract and I would not be representing my motherland at any beauty competitions.

It certainly hurt my feelings that Deepa never called back and, in hindsight, I realize I was probably up for the part of an extra and not the lead. Regardless, I did learn one extremely valuable lesson. Always take the other bastard's number. Always.

III

Roaring Twenties

One drink is never enough.
Or one boy for that matter.

NEGOTIATING SINGLEDOM

I found that 'growing up' required three things—a driver's licence, a job, and a group of friends who supported non-committed coitus. And in Bangalore—a city that the *Lonely Planet* guide described as 'not an obvious charmer but with a handful of interesting sights, as a tourist destination, it's not a dead loss'—I found all three.

My first proper job was as a sales executive at a hotel company. Every morning I would set out to work wrapped untidily in several yards of medium quality Kanjeevaram silk—the fabric of choice for budget conscious Indian grandmothers everywhere. It was a rule that all female staffers had to wear a sari, a rule that had to have been devised by someone who had never worn one. I was responsible, and I use this word lightly, for selling hotel room nights and conference packages to disinterested corporate honchos and their irritable secretaries.

I had no real-world experience and so I assume I got the job based on an interview with my then boss, Mr Ravi Pickle.

This job requires strong people skills. Do you have strong people skills?

Absolutely, I answered, thinking that 'people skills' meant that I could party and keep people entertained, a notion I have been disabused of thanks to the many frustrating years I have since spent in jobs that required this virtue.

If Ravi had asked instead *This job requires hard work and dedication—are you hard-working and dedicated?* and assuming

I had answered truthfully, I would not have been hired. But I wouldn't have answered anything truthfully. I was young and immature, with a misplaced sense of entitlement, and much like young, immature, entitled people everywhere, I came to the rapid conclusion that the job wasn't a good fit for me. Naturally, this wasn't based on any kind of sensible analysis but on the fact that I was being paid Rs 7,500 a month, a rather depressing sum even in 1995, and if that wasn't enough, a third of my meagre salary went towards a life insurance policy my dad forced on me so that I would learn the value of saving for the future.

I was infuriated with my father. First of all, my future involved getting married and being taken care of, and so it was obvious I would need all my money to buy nice clothes and shoes, and be seen at places where I could find this future provider. Plus, what twenty-three-year old needs a life insurance policy? Wasn't that for old people with responsibilities? Like my dad, for instance? The only reason I didn't put up the kind of fight I was usually capable of was because I lived at home with my parents and enjoyed all the perks such as no rent, no housework and no cooking that come with such an arrangement. The downside was that it placed me in a rather weak position when it came to any kind of negotiation that involved my folks and while I was most certainly ungrateful, I wasn't entirely stupid.

As far as I was concerned, my life was crap and the only thing I had going for me were my friends. Our main, or rather only, form of entertainment was drinking. And while the rest of the country referred to their drinking establishments as 'bars', we Bangaloreans called them 'pubs'—making them sound more like quiet spots in the city where one could be served a civilized drink rather than what they were, places with loud music, engulfed in cigarette smoke and with hordes of caterwauling twenty-somethings.

Each pub had its own distinct personality. The hardcore drinkers went to Take 5—a pub on Race Course Road and thus slightly removed from the main drag. It was where the 'been-there-done-that' type of person hung out, and where the women drank whisky. The pot-smoking drinkers went to Pico's, a place that had modelled itself after a Goa shack and catered to college students who were literally too cool for school and could regularly be seen smoking joints and drinking beer in the middle of the day. The pot-smoking drinkers who were into heavy metal—or what I considered alternative music—went to Purple Haze.

Growing up, these were the designated 'cool' places. But I wasn't cool, I was a nice middle-class girl seeking upward mobility, aka a yuppie, and because I was subconsciously seeking a yuppie-groom I had two options. Pub World was the first; a dark wood-and-plaid job that was actually kind of fly except that it was the 'civilian' joint that my dad and his friends usually chose if they absolutely had to go anywhere but the Armed Forces clubs for a drink. And so I ended up at The Black Cadillac, or 'BC' as it was called, which happened to have no personality at all. I know this may sound harsh, and quite frankly a little rich coming from someone who spent every single Friday and Saturday night there, and many weeknights too, but that was the case. BC was like Kim Kardashian—it was famous and fun and everyone wanted to be there but none of us were entirely clear why.

And so every Friday night I would swan in with my posse wearing what I always wore—high-waist Levi's 501s, a transparent wife-beater and penny loafers. On days that I wore anything more imaginative, it was borrowed. I would immediately locate and air-kiss one of my two beloved waiters—Valentine or Das, place my drink order, usually a large peg of whatever I had decided was 'my' drink of the moment, light up a Classic Mild and go in search of the DJ so that I could enjoy all of my favourite melodies including 'Mr Boombastic' by Shaggy, 'The Music Sounds Better with You' by Stardust and my beloved Whitney Houston's 'I'm Every Woman'—which I, needless to say, believed I was. Once I had consumed my first drink I would run around the bar saying hello to anyone I vaguely knew, although the volume of my greeting and the strength of my embrace would make anyone who didn't know us assume we were family.

HI! Where are we going after this? Whose party? I don't know him. Can I bring some people? Yes, yes they are all women—okay we'll see you there. HIIII!!!! Where have you been!? We are going to a party, do you want to come with us? Yes, you can bring people. Okay, we'll see you there. HIIII!

And so it went. My goal for Friday and Saturday night was to stay out as late as possible because that was the only way for me to judge how much fun I had had. A firm believer in quantity over quality, I wanted the night to last forever and quite often it felt like it did.

What's the matter with you? my father would ask on an average Sunday morning as I sat listlessly at the dining table trying not to hurl at the sight of two fried eggs.

Nothing, I'd lie feebly.

Look at this idiot, Mother, she looks sick. My dad calls my mother 'Mother' when he is snitching on me to her.

I'm not sick. I'm just tired, I would croak in response. The last thing I needed was for my parents to figure out that their daughter was the resident puke queen. Please don't let them find what I did in the flowerbed, I prayed, as I gingerly sipped on some water. Although the weekends were the greatest times of my life, they could have been even greater had it not been for one gigantic problem. When it came to alcohol consumption I was a lightweight.

It wasn't entirely my fault. My drinking practice focused on keeping costs down and my friends and I had figured out that drinking fast would provide the quickest buzz. The problem with this system, of course, was that it usually gave me the old I-am-having-the-time-of-my-life feeling for a rather limited amount of time, after which I would projectile vomit and pass out. Not willing to accept any responsibility for this I usually blamed the type of alcohol I'd had.

Beer doesn't agree with me, I would announce, as I flung one vodka shot after another down my gullet only to be met with the exact same result.

I even tried to blame the quality of the goods.

That Old Monk crap is the worst! were the last words I would remember screaming loudly before throwing up three perfectly good Bacardi dark rum and Coke combos.

Worried that my behaviour would impede what was essentially a man-search, I followed my friend Ruchika's advice and began 'sipping gently' on my drinks. Unfortunately, about halfway through the second drink I would forget to sip gently and by drink number four my friends had to help me stagger to the loo where I would do my worst.

I was disappointed in myself. From a genetic standpoint I should have been able to knock 'em back like the next man. My dad is from Goa and I shouldn't have to say much more—but for those of you who are not aware, Goans can drink pretty much anyone under the table. If we had a drinking contest in India the Goan representative would win. And if he or she lost, it would be to a Kodava—another tribe of maniacal drinkers. My mother is half Kodava. I am essentially three-quarters alcohol yet I was unable to get past four drinks. Regardless of my drinking disability I managed to have a brilliant time careening madly from one weekend to the next.

My dad remained steadfastly unimpressed with all of this.

How come you buggers have to make twenty phone calls every bloody Friday night to figure out where the hell you are going when you go to the same damn place every damn time?

It was true. My friends and I were usually so wound up by Friday afternoon with the excitement of getting drunk and possibly making out with some strange, or known, man that we would start calling each other at about 3 p.m. from our respective workplaces. It was imperative to know what everyone would be wearing, who else would be there and, the most critical part of the equation, how were we to get there and back?

In a country where public transport is at best horribly unsafe and at worst non-existent, we women are the ones who get stuck with the shit end of the stick. And unless you were a rich girl with a car and a driver, or a lucky girl with a brother or generous parent who would drive you, or a very pretty one with a boyfriend, you were screwed.

I was screwed and so my modus operandi was to find out which of my friends had a ride, a task that involved between three to eight phone calls, then taking an autorickshaw to her home while it was still bright outside, and shower and change there. More often than not I was one of about five other girls with the same idea, thus giving the car we were eventually transported in the undignified look of an overcrowded village taxi. Naturally, the driver of the car was not obliged to drop us home although I was always so friendly and grateful that the driver quite often did not have the heart to ditch me at the end of the evening. On the rare occasion that I did have to fend for myself I would usually just latch on to a friend's boyfriend. These guys were truly the easiest targets because they would do anything to get laid, including dropping their girlfriends' friends to the furthest and most far-flung neighbourhoods of Bangalore.

My dad, of course, selfishly cared about none of this.

So what if you can't go out? What do you suppose will happen to you if you spend one weekend at home?

I will die, I wanted to say, because I am not a loser. Only losers, with big red Ls on their foreheads, stay home on weekends and survive the trauma.

She'll probably explode, he said to no one in particular,

answering his own idiotic question. *Anyway just stay off the phone, it's my official phone, don't forget.*

As if on cue the phone rang and I jumped to get it, grabbing the receiver before it could ring twice.

Hi Anj! Yes I am leaving right now, should be at your place by seven. Can I eat there? Great, thanks. And do you think Gautam can drop me home too?

As if it was any of his business, my dad who was still lurking around eavesdropping on my conversation leapt in.

What sort of friends do you have, he would spit, *if the lot of you spends half your time begging for a lift?*

The sort, I silently raged, who have irritating bloody parents like you who won't let them drive the family car at night.

And on the rare occasion that I did have a ride from my doorstep, *What sort of guy pulls up in front of the house and toots his horn? How come your friends never come in? And, more to the point, what sort of person are you who goes running off with these people?*

'These people', I wanted to inform him, 'were the kind of guys who, like me, were in a tearing hurry to get going so we could get a drink as quickly as possible'. In all likelihood they had come quite far out of their way to fetch me and, if I got very lucky, would drop me home at 3.30 a.m. without the expectation of a hand-job. 'And the reason no one wants to come in is because you people are boring'. I was usually rescued from this line of questioning by the sound of my friend Suro's horn and I would grab my keys, yell goodnight to my mum and scuttle off. Sometimes, however, Suro was late, and the horn I had heard belonged to my neighbour's ride. On those nights I would have to skulk back into the house and right into my father's gleefully smirking face.

And, speaking of coming back into the house, once my parents had gone to bed re-entry into the Vaz home became a complicated thing. My parents' home has a boundary wall and gate that is about five-and-a-half feet high. Yet, they believed that locking the gate would act as an effective deterrent to thieves who might be plotting to steal my mother's far-from-prize-winning papayas. For reasons unknown to me my parents decided that I only deserved a key to the front door and so, in order to get back into the compound, I was expected to vault over the gate. At 4 a.m. I was an undignified sight as I attempted to clamber over the gate in a series of unattractive contortions made even more awful because of my advanced state of inebriation. I would fumble about, desperately trying to keep my balance, while also trying not to clonk myself in the clitoris. The fact that any man, after seeing this performance, actually came back for seconds is a testament to how difficult it was in 1995 to meet a single woman who would willingly put out. In the front seat of a car.

But no matter what impediments stood in the way of having a good time I was able to overcome them and, in general, life was amazing. Although every now and again inquiring aunties would remind me that there was a future that I had to tend to.

Don't you have a boyfriend? they would ask, frowns firmly in place. And then, much more to the point, *When are you getting married?*

And, of course, they had questions! Because while my generation helped push the 'marriageable age' from twenty to thirty and the age for childbirth with 'additional risks' to forty, all we had really done was move the timeline, we were still expected to marry. How else could we prove our worth as women if no one picked us to be a wife?

And why wouldn't I want marriage? After all, I had been given to understand that my wedding day would be the happiest and thinnest day of my life, topped only by the birth of my children. No matter where I looked, that was the message. Look around you! To this day, is there a movie you can think of where the happy ending is that she remains single? *Working Girl*, a classic 1980s film about female financial independence and ambition, made sure its heroine found love at the end—with fucking Indiana Jones no less; *Pretty Woman*, also a film about female financial independence and ambition, ended with a hooker landing an officer and a gentleman, and more recently *Bridesmaids* did it too. Conversely what happens to single women? Three words: *Thelma and Louise*—the moment they divest themselves of their male counterparts they die, but before that one almost gets raped and both get robbed. In other words, it doesn't end well. I was going to have to step up my efforts and seal the deal.

DESPERATE WOMEN DO DESPERATE THINGS

It was a regular Saturday night. Swati, Gayathri and I had spoken multiple times during the day and the plan was to meet at my hotel around 7 p.m. where, as part of a sales training exercise, I was spending the week in a rather nice guest room. Technically, I was done with my rotation and could have gone home but given the proximity of the hotel to The Black Cadillac I realized it was in my best interest to stay put. Gayathri had managed to get her dad to drop her there and Swati had agreed to come get us since she had her dad's car for the evening.

My dad! Gayathri groaned as soon as she entered my room while fishing deep in her bag for a packet of smokes and a bottle of Old Monk that she had probably stolen from her dad. *He has lost it.*

They all have, I offered, *mine wanted to know what would happen if I stayed in on a weekend.*

Ewww, Gayathri wrinkled her nose like I had just farted.

Exactly, I told him to fuck off. Both G and I knew I had told him nothing of the sort. But it was the thought that counted. *Swati is so lucky her parents are divorced.*

At which point reception called to inform me that Swati was on her way up to my room. I opened the door to let her in.

My bloody dad didn't give me the car! she yelled loud enough for the entire floor to have heard.

What! Why?

He had to go somewhere last minute.

What! That's so unfair. Fucking parents, man! What the hell are we supposed to do now?

Thanks to the fact that we didn't have far to go, and to the fact that there were three of us, hence safety in numbers, we decided to take an autorickshaw. By this time we had had a drink or two, our shitty parents were a long forgotten memory, and this night ride in an auto-rickshaw was beginning to feel like a bit of an adventure. We jumped in and told the driver where to drop us.

The thing about an auto is that while it is a perfectly acceptable mode of transport it is most certainly not the yuppie woman's chariot of choice, especially not for an evening out.

Tell him to make sure he drops us at the crossing. I don't want him dropping us right in front of BC, I instructed Gayathri. Our image and reputation were at stake after all.

But because it appeared that all the men in our lives were conspiring to screw us over, the auto driver completely ignored our request, and instead of stopping at the crossing, he revved his engine, bringing us to a stop right in front of BC in a cloud of exhaust fumes. In a fit of extreme embarrassment we disgorged ourselves from his vehicle giving him more money than he deserved because none of us wished to be seen waiting around for change.

Do I smell of the auto? I asked nervously, as we marched in pretending we were better than people who regularly used autos and hoping that none of the good-looking guys had seen us in it.

Despite this perceived humiliation, we managed to rally pretty quickly and soon the evening was back on track. I was busy chatting with my friend Kabir when this guy walked up to us. He knew Kabir from boarding school and it was clear the two had not met in a while. Kabir introduced us using my first name and his last name which I didn't catch because I was too busy checking him out.

I was immediately interested for two reasons. First, he was

cute. And, second, he was from out of town. I particularly liked out-of-towners, and this one lived in Hubli, a town we Bangalore people disparagingly considered the boonies. But I liked guys from the boonies. They didn't intimidate me, and were far easier to please because they seemed happy just to be in an actual city where the women weren't afraid to talk to them. And I certainly wasn't afraid to talk—the problem with talking, however, is that at some point you wind up saying things that you will regret.

You should try the brunch buffet at The Oberoi, I gushed, when he asked for suggestions on where to spend the following morning, *the spread is rather eclectic.*

I was doing a few things here. I was being worldly by suggesting brunch instead of a boring old lunch; I had also indicated that I belonged to a certain socio-economic bracket having actually experienced a meal at a five-star hotel coffee shop; and I had used the word 'eclectic' that I had recently learnt and that made me sound intelligent. I could have used 'amazing' or 'fantastic' but I had not.

The chicken biryani is to die for. Once again I had killed two birds with one stone. While I was Miss Fancy-Schmancy-eating-brunch-at-The-Oberoi, I was still a down-to-earth girl who liked her chicken biryani. I was approachable but classy. I had also thrown in 'to die for', a phrase I came to loathe about a year later due to its overuse by my peers in the hotel industry when it came to describing any kind of culinary experience. But at that moment it was new to me and sounded grown-up. Rather akin to 'let's do lunch'.

And the appams and stew. Taking Kabir and his silence as a sign that I should go through the entire 'eclectic' line-up of food, I was on a roll.

And the pineapple cream cake. Have you tried that?! I directed this at Kabir who had not tried the cake. *Oh, that is something else. It's…it's…* damn, I had already used up 'eclectic' and 'to die for'—*it's divine, DE-VINE is what it is. I ate so much of it. Three slices I think, and they are large slices by the way, about this big*—I picked up a napkin and folded it into the exact size of a fucking pineapple pastry. *It was so creamy, with all these layers, I would have eaten even more except that I finally threw up.* WHAT! What was I saying? But I couldn't stop. *Luckily it wasn't induced vomiting, though, that's the worst, this was just—you know—it was a reflex and I felt much better after.* We stood around in silence for a bit, Kabir and the stranger had no way to respond to what they had just heard. Why had I just told him I had puked pineapple cream cake? Why did I think this story would benefit my chances of appearing attractive? It wasn't even a funny story, this wasn't a punch line. No it was me blithering on because I was too nervous to stop. Which is how I realized I had a big old-fashioned crush on this man. I wanted to rewind and start over.

Thankfully, Kabir did the next best thing, which was to swiftly change the topic, *Do you guys have plans for later?* By 'guys' he meant my girlfriends. Ah! A life raft to a drowning woman. *Yes!* I squealed, grateful for this deliverance, *We are going to The Club.* The Club, while rather unimaginatively named, was actually a lot of fun. It had a massive outdoor area with two bars and a small sound-proof dance floor with pretty good music. We would dance until we dripped with sweat, go out to dry off and then come back in. This would be done until closing time. *We were thinking of The Orion,* I could not help trying to show off my insider status, *but The Club will be open later.*

With that I pretended I had to go talk to other people. When it was time for us to leave I made sure to find Kabir and my new friend. *Are you guys coming?* I asked, hoping that my tone was a balance of friendly and welcoming rather than desperate and desperate. They were, Kabir assured me. Perfect—nothing like alcohol, loud music and very low lighting to move things along. I still couldn't remember his name though and now I had passed the point of being able to ask again without coming off as an asshole. It is a fact that one has a very small window of opportunity to clarify a person's name, usually about a minute after being first introduced. My window had slammed shut. I would have to wait until I heard Kabir refer to him, which he steadfastly refused to do.

Once there, we danced and drank, and drank and danced and sweated. Everyone was having a great time. I put on the best dance performance ever—which consisted mainly of moves that I imagined women in the sex trade industry would make. We were getting along very well, and thanks to the loud music I wasn't able to talk and embarrass myself further. At 3 a.m. it was time to locate the girls.

Did anything happen? Gayathri had assumed that with all the gymnastics I had put myself through on the dance floor I would have at least got to base two.

Nothing. At all.

What's wrong with you? Fair question.

Vaz! What happened? Swati had joined us.

Nothing happened, Gayathri answered for me, *because she is a stupid ass.* It wasn't that Gayathri thought I was actually stupid; she was angry because as a rule we all lived vicariously through one another, her victories were mine and vice-versa. A night like this wasn't just a disappointment for me, it was a let-down for my friends because now we had absolutely nothing to discuss when we woke up the next day.

Swati, at least, was sympathetic. *Don't worry Vaz, we still have some booze left in the room and Dhruva will drop us back. I begged him.* Dhruva was her cousin who sometimes took pity on us.

As we were leaving, and as I was thinking all was lost, I heard someone call my name. Playing it cool, I went over to say goodnight to Kabir and the new guy. Kabir very discreetly left us alone, saying he was going to get one last drink. We stood there awkwardly as if waiting for Kabir to return—I had decided to say nothing seeing how successful I had been earlier in the evening. And then something that had NEVER ever happened to me happened. He asked me out to lunch the next day. He was leaving town the following night so could he please have lunch with me. I was stunned. It was the first time anyone had tried to feed me before trying to fuck me. He was treating me like a lady. I agreed at once and gave him my number after which I triumphantly stalked off and out of The Club, with Gayathri, Swati and Dhruva all following me, eager for the details, which I regaled them with all the way back to the hotel.

The next morning I woke up in a complete panic at 8 a.m.

Wake up! I yelled at Gayathri, who had stayed the night.

Why?! she groaned, from under the covers.

I have to get home. I gave him my number and he is going to call, I can't miss the call. Hurry, we have to get out of here.

Nobody is going to call this early, said Gayathri infuriated. She had taken the trouble to sit up to tell me this.

How do you know? He may be an early bird. We know nothing about him.

Including his name apparently.

This was true but I ignored her sarcasm.

He will introduce himself when he calls. Now move it!

For two women, we managed to break every record by clearing out of the room in less than twenty minutes and I was home by 9 a.m.

I walked in to find my dad sitting there having a leisurely chat on the phone with some pal.

Can you please get off the phone, I whispered as silently and politely as possible, *I am expecting a phone call.*

I don't care, my father mouthed back to me.

My dad was doing this on purpose and I was forced to suffer through the next several minutes.

Look, I announced to both my parents as soon as he was done, *I met a guy last night and he is taking me out for lunch.*

What does that have to do with my phone? When talking to me my father had started to use possessive pronouns when mentioning the house or anything in it.

Because he has to tell me what time to meet him.

If he is so very keen to see you maybe he will try calling back if the line is busy.

I can't take that chance, I answered honestly, before planting myself right next to the telephone.

Just as I said this, the phone rang and I nearly jumped out of my skin.

Hello! I answered, hoping that all the cigarette smoking had given my voice a Demi Moore effect.

Bertie? the voice at the other end asked, *do you have a cold?*

I recognized the voice to be that of my dad's friend Roy Kothavala, someone I was usually happy to chat with because he loved to share his filthiest jokes with me. But not today, plus I was annoyed that he thought I sounded like my dad.

No, Uncle Roy, I said clearing my throat, *it's Radhika. He isn't here, can he call you back? Yes, I am fine. No, I do not have a cold. Yes, he will call back. Bye.*

I looked up at the smug faces of both my parents.
RING RING.

Now it was my turn to be smug. I lifted the receiver.

Hello. Please dear God, do not let me sound man-ish.

Vaz?

Swati?

Why are you sounding so weird? Has he called?

No, he hasn't, and can you please not call till later, what if he is trying right now?

Why are you whispering?

Because my fucking dad is lurking around.

Okay, okay, call me when he calls.
Yes, yes, bye.

What was wrong with everyone? What if he had called while I was on the phone? I had no way of knowing, and even though I knew the name of the hotel he was staying at, I certainly couldn't call him. It would look desperate, even by my low standards, and I didn't have his room number, or, as we all know, his name.

I finally peeled myself away to bathe but not before strictly instructing my parents to stay off the horn and if he did call while I was in the loo to please come and get me. This was a phone call I was prepared to take with shampoo in my hair and soap suds in my eyes.

Turns out he wasn't an early bird and so when he finally did call, at noon, I had almost given up.

Hello.

Hi, can I speak to Radhika please. It was him!

This is Radhika, I said, cool as ice as if I had no clue who it was.

Hi—it's Thakran, we met last night.

Oh hi! I replied, relieved I finally had a name. *How are you?*

I'm fine, slightly hung-over, are you still free for lunch?

Yes, yes, of course, I said, abandoning my cool-as-ice vibe.

We decided to meet at Casa Piccola, Bangalore's answer to Rome, known far and wide for its highly spiced version of Italian fare. Once there, I decided to try and charm him with my communication skills.

I love the profiteroles. Have you ever eaten a profiterole? We have to order the profiteroles, I insisted before launching into a lengthy description of a profiterole. *It's basically a whole pile of chocolate éclairs—with whipped cream and chocolate sauce poured on top of it and then if you like you can get some ice cream on the side and have them pour chocolate sauce on that as well. It's delicious—I can't stop eating it.*

By this point he was probably expecting me to tell him I had vomited those up as well. And so in an effort to keep my mouth shut I asked him a few questions and like a good Indian I decided I first needed to find out where he was from.

Haryana, he said. Ooh! A one-word-answer guy. How nice.

I had heard of Haryana, of course; what I did not know then was that it was, and still is, one of the most oppressively feudal and chauvinistic states in our country with just about the worst gender discrimination you will find. But how could I have known any of this, busy as I was not reading newspapers or books.

My parents live in a place called Gurgaon.
I have heard of that, I said proudly.
They moved there before we were born.
And who is 'we'?
My three older brothers. They live in a joint family.
Where did they move from?
The village.

Now I was really listening. This guy was a proper Indian. Talk about belonging! He had a monosyllabic answer to the first, all-important 'where are you from', and his folks were from a village! And suddenly I was transported back to 1978—I was five and it was the year I met Roopinder.

My parents are pretty conventional, my mother speaks Hindi—no English.

Wow, I thought, just like Roopinder's. And then, unbeknownst to him, he threw in the clincher that would make sure he got laid.

She keeps a cow in her backyard.

Holy shit! This guy *was* Roopinder. Okay, it was a cow not a herd of buffaloes but still, let's be honest, he was a quadruple threat.

All my life I had wanted to be Roopinder, consciously at first and then at a more subconscious level. I had, over the years, come to accept I could not be her, but now here I was sitting in Casa Piccola, face-to-face with the possibility of marrying her. Yes, yes,

I had spent my life searching for Roopinder and her family, and now it looked like I had found them and it was going to take a lot to pry them from my sticky fingers. By the end of our meal I had convinced myself that we were already a couple of sorts—of course, there were some loose ends that needed tying up but it was clear to me. We were to be married.

Back then—just like Mariah Carey—I too had a vision of love. A vision of a relationship that everyone else would covet. We would only be apart during office hours. You could not think of me without thinking of him and vice versa. We would flit from one romantic meal to another. My life would be clogged with flowers and cards. He would be infatuated with me. Without me, his life would not be worth living, every breath would seem an exercise in futility. I would be his everything. I would be his all.

DETERMINED TO MARRY

I was hardwired to want marriage. I never wondered why I would want it, what the benefit of such a union was—none of that. No, I was just conditioned to think this was part of my future. Several of my close friends had got married and I was starting to feel a little left out of this glamorous-looking club, the membership of which meant you could live rent-free. It wasn't a complete fantasy, though. I did have a boyfriend; we just didn't discuss marriage, the future, or for that matter the next day. If I was going to close this deal then I was going to have to do it step by logical step and my first order of business was to pry an 'I love you' out of him.

This, of course, like quitting smoking or Facebook, was easier said than done. Part of the problem may have been that I am not an 'I love you' type of person, I wasn't raised by 'I love you' people. The closest my parents and I have come is 'lots of love' which we say in a hurried and muffled manner, so that in a court of law one would be hard-pressed to prove that it was said at all. I was, and still am, one of those people who is embarrassed by the word love, yet here I was desperate to hear it. And because these words had not been spoken, I spent every waking moment analysing why. I would plumb the depths of every word, facial expression and hand gesture for meaning. And helping me analyse all this was Anuli whom I would call eleventy times a day.

I just got off the phone with him, I whispered to her from my desk at the office. *He was so abrupt. It's the end.*

What did he say, tell me exactly? This is why girlfriends are so important; they allow you to relive moments and details that are boring as hell to anyone other than yourself. The therapeutic value of this is immeasurable and I feel genuinely sorry for women who don't have girlfriends in their lives. How do they cope?!

Nothing, he just answered my questions in monofuckingsyllables and then he said goodbye.

Did you call him or did he call you?

I called him. Oh my god, I shouldn't have. That is why he was abrupt, he thinks I am despo. Which I was; I just didn't want to transmit that message to him.

He doesn't think you are despo, he just isn't a phone person.

What do you mean he isn't a phone person What is that? It's just an excuse.

No, no—it's not. My Aunt El Nora is not a phone person, she hates the phone, I am telling you, it's a real thing.

I wasn't convinced.

I have an idea! What if I call him? If he is abrupt with me then we know that he isn't a phone person. This was genius.

Call me back as soon as you speak to him, I said, and slammed down the receiver. I then proceeded to wait tensely by the phone hoping a client wouldn't call until my crisis had passed.

Ten minutes later Anuli called back.

What happened? I was almost afraid to ask.

Well, Anuli said, fighting to keep her voice neutral, *he was pretty chatty actually but...*

I wasn't going to let her make any excuses for him. *See, he is a fucking phone person! Just not with me.*

I was in hell. However, like a manic-depressive, I dangled precariously between wanting to die and giddy elation. This was evidenced that very evening when we all went out for drinks. Thaks introduced me to a friend of his as his girlfriend and I went off the deep end, I preened and strutted around the entire evening.

The next morning Anuli and I were on our daily update.
What do you think he meant when he said 'girlfriend'?
That you are his girlfriend. I wanted to smack Anuli, she knew just as well as I did that in love there are no easy answers.
Yes, but do you think he meant it as 'this is the girl who I am in love with girlfriend', or did he mean 'this is not a serious relationship girlfriend'?
He meant the first one.
Do you think his friends understood it like that?
I don't know, came her patient response.
See! I cried, *this is why men need to be clear. Nobody understands anything they say.*

I finally decided that actions spoke louder than words. My birthday was around the corner and, sure, while things had been casual thus far something told me (probably another Hollywood film) that this day would be special. I mean, no matter where you are from, you would literally have to be Helen Keller to not know how important the first birthday is in a relationship, and even she, as we know, had probably figured it out. Keeping my luck in mind I kept my expectations low. I expected a card, and I fantasized that it would be funny and he would have been forced to scrawl a few words of endearment in it. I hoped for a gift as well, nothing big, just a token of his affection. He had given me absolutely nothing so far so it made complete sense that he would make a grand gesture on my birthday.

It annoyed me no end that my idiot birthday was on a weekday. I resented the fact that everyone had work the following morning and that the idea of having to wake up the next day would ensure that, while an enjoyable evening would be had, it would not be an all-out rager. Also, Thaks would not be drunk enough to accidentally make any rash commitment. The silver lining on this otherwise bleak cloud was that Anuli had gone gift shopping. I immediately jumped to the conclusion that my loved one had put her up to this task—because that is what guys do, they hire their girlfriend's BFF to buy gifts.

We gathered at our friend Hazy's apartment for pre-going out drinks. As is customary, everyone made much of me, which was a bit annoying because I was unable to judge if Thaks was behaving any differently. I was also very distracted because I kept wondering when I would be given my gifts. Turned out there was just one—a beautiful silver chain that, based on the look on everyone's face, including Thaks', they had all chipped in to buy.

This is exactly what I wanted, I squealed with as much false cheer as I could muster. This was going to be one long night. I smiled through the pain while simultaneously pinning my hopes on Valentine's Day.

A word about Valentine's Day. It is, in my opinion, the dumbest day of the year. I think it was invented with the sole purpose of making all the popular people feel even more popular, and for the rest of us to feel even more inadequate. If you had a life that was generally dull, predictable and colourless, then Valentine's Day was created to remind you of that lest you had managed to forget it.

But I put aside my differences with Valentine's Day and decided that for once I would not be my usual cynical self. I would instead work with St. Val and the Universe towards a positive outcome. And so, on the morning of 14 February, I awoke not with a sense of trepidation but with a feeling that something great was about to happen. I received confirmation from my parents that nothing had been delivered to the house. No flowers? Were they absolutely sure? Yes, they were. No worries, he would be sending them to the office.

I marched into the office, the reception area of which offered a clean view of my work space, and there sitting on my desk was a beautifully arranged pot of red roses. I could not believe it! Positive thinking had never ever done me any good before; in fact, I didn't believe in it at all, but here was the proof! I rushed to my desk along with Liv and Asha, my boss's assistants, who had been kept abreast of the state of my relationship and hence were at least as excited as I was because they knew the significance of such a gift. I reached for the card and opened it with a flourish.

'Happy happy! See you guys when I am back from Coorg. Cheers! Apu.'

I thought I was having a heart attack. Apu, a close friend, contaminated from his time spent in the US of A, where just about everyone sends everyone else a Valentine's Day greeting, had taken it up on himself to send me flowers. A purely platonic gesture that was confirmed within minutes via a phone call from Anuli.

Did you get flowers from Apu?
Yes, I answered listlessly.
Me too! Isn't he a sweetie?

No, I thought, he is not a sweetie, he is an imbecile. Does he have any idea what he just did?

Naturally, things didn't end there and I stumbled along like this for several months. I was on an emotional rollercoaster ride from hell and it was entirely of my own making. This was the victim-type behaviour that I nowadays admonish my young nieces to never ever indulge in because it is shameful and embarrassing to the entire female species. But there I was shaming us all. I always wished I could have been a proud woman who did not let anything get to her; instead I was the antithesis of such a female. I had zero pride. If anything I had less than zero pride, my pride levels had managed to sink to a negative number.

In the course of that year two of my close friends got married. Weren't weddings supposed to soften the hardest of hearts? Weren't they meant to inspire love? Why wasn't he inspired by all this when I was so clearly out of my mind with inspiration? I was fed-up, I was going to tell him that he either had to get serious and let me know when we were getting married, or it was over. My way or the highway. I would behave like a proud woman, holding my head high.

I discussed this plan with all the girls and they agreed that it was a wise one, and quite possibly the only one that would provide me, and them, with any peace. I was feeling extremely confident about my decision until Anuli brought something to my attention that I hadn't yet considered.

Listen, Vaz, are you prepared for him to choose the highway?

What do you mean?

You know—it's a big decision for anyone. In fact, he may just choose the highway for lack of knowing what else to do.

It was clear she was trying to soften what was essentially a left hook, right upper cut to my plan. And put like that it was clear I had no plan at all. I was not in the least bit prepared to see him choose the highway. If he did choose it I knew I would fold immediately, thus making myself look utterly pathetic.

Plus, Vaz, it's December. Christmas, New Year's…I don't know if this is great timing.

She was right. This was rubbish timing. Studies have shown that suicides spike dramatically during the holidays and I suspect they are all committed by people who gave their significant other's ultimatums. There would be no ultimatums; I would rather suffer through a sub-standard relationship than kill myself.

Then, a few months later, as if testing my resolve, I was given the piece of news that he was moving to America.

I got into Columbia, isn't that great?!

If there is anything more tiresome than pretending you are happy for someone when you are not, I would like to know what that is.

I was now convinced I would be dying alone and so the first thing I did when I had a moment to myself was locate my John Denver tape. I fast-forwarded to 'Leaving on a Jet Plane' and spent the next few hours immersed in self-pity. John Denver is great for this type of thing because even his happy songs are sad. I first became familiar with his work as a child and I developed a soft spot for 'Leaving on a Jet Plane' when my parents dumped me in boarding school—the feeling of abandonment that followed my initial enthusiasm was perfectly articulated in the lyrics and mournful tune.

Once I had exhausted myself in this manner I began to visualize the end of the relationship that was no doubt rapidly approaching. Emotionally I vacillated between Gloria Gaynor's 'I Will Survive' whenever I felt hopeful and upbeat, and Diana Ross's 'Touch Me in the Morning' when I felt like the need to be a martyr but also the need for a disco beat.

They say adversity brings out the best in people. In my case it brought out the pettiest. I found myself rejoicing every time he experienced some setback.

What! The American Consulate rejected your visa application because you didn't take the TOEFL?

On the other hand, I was in hell when things went well.

Your friend Lokesh found out that you can take the exam in Singapore next weekend?

I now hated Lokesh, a man I had never met.

I was unable to enjoy the last few weeks of togetherness because I was preoccupied with how much worse I would feel when he left. And then he did. Naturally I had John Denver do overtime until every mucous membrane in my body was dehydrated. Thanks to his melancholic music I was able to view my situation in the worst possible light. I had been left behind. I would never meet another man again. My life stretched out endlessly and emptily in front of me.

My friends tried tough love. *Vaz, have you not heard of the old saying 'If you love someone set them free'?*

Of course I had heard of it, I thought it was an extremely

depressing idea. Especially the second half of this tiresome phrase which goes something like 'if they come back to you then they are yours to hold, if not then it was never meant to be'. So if I understood this correctly I was supposed to set something free that could then fly around with god-only-knows-who and then IF it felt like it then it could come back to me? No thanks! The fact of the matter was that people who lived in glasshouses did throw stones, we all cried over spilt milk and there were far too many examples of folks reaping far more than they sowed. This was all bullshit. I wasn't setting anything free.

Eventually I grew immune to Mr Denver and I began to think. I pondered every single comment, conversation, email, and phone call we ever had. And as I mulled over all this I realized that while he had moved to the other side of the planet, from a technical standpoint he had not broken up with me. An idea began to brew in my brain.

Most single Indian women are willing to uproot themselves and move 7,000 miles from home with no money, no clear professional advantage, and no family for one of two reasons. The first is ambition, a hunger for something more than what she already has— to broaden her horizons as it were. The second is for a man who loves her and who has promised he will marry her— she is already in possession of a ring and possibly of a marriage licence as well. I was moving for a third reason that had as yet not been invented, for a man who hadn't said he loved me but had also not categorically stated that he did not. For all that I put my friends, myself and John Denver through, I was going to give this relationship every chance it had. I was going to marry this person and I was going to America to do it.

IV

Hello 'Merica!

An Indian in the cold.

PLEASE LET ME IN

Conventional wisdom, and the experiences of many friends before me, had shown that I would have the best chance of surviving the prairie if I went there as a student. It was the smart thing to do; I could get myself an American degree, thus qualifying me for an American job, plus the idea of being a student greatly appealed to my inherently lazy mindset. Student life, in my experience, was way better than working a job and I quite looked forward to regressing into the soft, warm, irresponsible world of childhood.

The only blight on the horizon was the dreaded GRE, an exam that involved mathematical computations, something I was physically afraid of and had been psychologically scarred by pretty much right through school. The thought of having to calculate the square footage of a polygon sends cold shivers up and down my spine and equations make me want to vomit. To this day, I have recurring nightmares about math exams. What I am trying to say is that all this fear and hard work was rather a lot for me to contemplate. Nonetheless I was in love and motivated by a far greater fear than algebra—the fear that my boyfriend would get to New York only to be seduced by a woman from Sidney Sheldon's *Other Side of Midnight*.

The first step in my American expedition was to identify the universities I could go to. I needed to find a graduate programme that would be easy to get into, easy to get financial aid for and, above all, easy to graduate from with high grades because, let's be honest, I wasn't going to America to tax myself—that I could do by staying put in India in my job where I was kicked around daily by my crappy client. I knew I was putting in a tall order, but as my friend Farhad Madon told me when we were in the eighth grade, *aim for the stars, fall in the trees*. This was in relation to our forthcoming final exam for which neither of us had studied. Anyway, motivational speakers from Oprah Winfrey down have always said 'dream big or not at all' and this was what I intended to do.

In my mind, the first stop I would need to make was at the American consulate office in Chennai. Being a fan of 'Merica, I was naturally a fan of the consulate building and had been curious about it ever since I first arrived in Chennai a few months earlier to start a new job. It was located close to my office and was built to resemble a maximum-security prison, except this one was built to keep the natives outside. What went on behind those walls, I would wonder, and now finally I had every bloody reason to find out. As a prospective student I would need to visit the student centre where the hours of operation matched perfectly with my own office hours. Being a natural born liar, I informed my boss that I had a major problem with my landlady and had to go meet with her. I didn't say what the problem was but I did what I could to project the fear and helplessness one might feel if one was to be evicted for no fault of theirs. And then I skipped out of my office in a state of high excitement as if I were already on my way to New York City.

When I got to the consulate I found out that in order to gain entry into the compound one had to divest oneself of all electronic gadgets and bags. The only items allowed in, besides some form of identification and a small wallet/purse, were a pen or pencil and notepaper. If I wanted to get into the consulate that day I was informed I would have to leave my handbag on the sidewalk. This was all rather anti-climactic to say the least, but I was in

America now so there would be no rule-bending. I went back to work with a story about my awful, villainous landlady who had cancelled on me at the last minute. Of course I now know that bosses believe nothing you say no matter how believable you may think it is but all this was information I was yet to come by and, in my innocence, I imagined I had fooled her properly.

The next day when I set off to visit my 'landlady' I hoped my boss would not notice I was leaving without my handbag and instead had ten sheets of paper from the office printer under my arm. This time I was admitted into the hallowed grounds after signing the visitors' book and being frisked for firearms. I know that many of my Indian friends resented this whole procedure, *Who do these fucking Americans think they are? They need to remember they are on Indian soil, if anything we should be searching them!* They wanted to study and live in America but found the security check to be insulting, *Americans are fucking paranoid. They go around poking their noses in everyone's business and then when everyone wants to kill them I have to suffer this shit!* I would keep quiet during such discussions because, unlike my countrymen, I rather welcomed the whole cloak-and-dagger vibe. By adding my name to the visitors' book, I felt like I had just signed on for the start of my mission—there was something very inaugural about it. I felt like this was America's first step in welcoming me into the fold, although the frisking itself may have been a tad paranoid. For one thing I was wearing very tight pants so really where would I be hiding anything? And, for another, I was a fan, I came in peace, I loved Dolly Parton. But they didn't know all that yet so I forgave them.

Once I got past the gates I was directed to the student centre. I had thought one of the guards would walk me to the building but instead he just waved me in the general direction of where I had to go and turned back to his radio, leaving me to my own devices. My god, I thought, I had the run of the place. I could be a spy for all they knew. Good thing I wasn't. Maybe I should complain to the authorities that their security wasn't tight enough. Maybe they would give me admission to college based on this selfless act alone.

I found the student centre at the end of a long, empty corridor. It was a high-ceilinged, cool, darkish room attached to a reference library that smelt musty. This, I thought, as I took in a lungful of airborne fungus, is what American universities must smell like. There were several Indians in there, all working feverishly at computer terminals or leafing through massive files filled with college brochures. Up until that point I had not seen any actual Americans, the guards being Indian as well. I will admit this was a bit disappointing, kind of like going to a party and finding out that the guy you are there to see is the only one who didn't show up.

And then I saw her! She was older, probably in her 60s, with light blue hair, and a kind, bespectacled face. Her outfit was far less fashionable than I would have expected, her mid-calf length skirt and synthetic blouse with a big, floppy bow at the neck reminding me more of a nun or missionary rather than an emissary from the land that gave us Pamela Anderson and Virginia Slims cigarettes. But she seemed solid and gave me the impression that she would take care of me, and shepherd me all the way to the land of milk and honey.

In truth, she was there to explain the facilities available at the centre—the computers were for people like me to practice the bothersome GRE test and the less bothersome TOEFL exam on, and the library had information on every single course available on every last university campus. I could photocopy anything I wanted to, of course, or take notes with my pen and notepaper that the security men had so kindly allowed me to bring in.

As an experienced procrastinator I had put the GRE and my fear of it out of mind and so I attacked the college brochures with enthusiasm. Within minutes I was lost in the fantasy of American education. Harvard, Berkeley, Texas A&M, Oberlin, Mount Holyoke, University of Iowa, Penn State. I had heard all these names before but looking at the pamphlets made it real! American colleges were fantastic and, from my current vantage point, looked positively luxurious. The cafeterias were not bleak like mine had been, they had buffets of food lined up and down, and all the athletic, gorgeous students sat about eating and drinking. Speaking of athletes, every school boasted gymnasiums I had no idea existed. I could already see my new, sinewy body slicing through a swimming pool or shimmying gracefully down a rock-wall. Naturally, I made no notes on any of the courses and so technically I was no closer to my goal than I had been when I signed in that morning. But this did not faze me. I would be back for more serious work in a day or two, and there was no sense in rushing any of this only to risk early burnout.

I was flying high with the excitement of having got the process started and possibly from the amount of mould that had entered my system, and was on my way out of the centre with a distinct skip in my step when Old Blue Hair stopped me. *Thought you might need this, dear*, she said handing me a photocopied sheet of something. It turned out to be a long list of all the documents I would need in order to get my student visa approved. Oh shit, I thought, coming back to earth with a painful thud, the bloody American visa.

Part of the joy of being Indian is being an Indian passport holder. An Indian passport holder never makes a spontaneous travel plan that involves an international destination. No matter how adventurous we may be at heart we cannot leap into a taxi, speed off to the airport and decide where we want to go when we get to the ticketing counter. An Indian passport holder needs a minimum of one month's notice for international travel, if not more, because we need a visa to go practically anywhere.

The whole visa situation is nothing but a damn nuisance. I would listen enviously to friends who held passports from other countries as they told stories of last-minute getaways, *we just decided last minute, like yesterday, that we were going to Spain and here we are.* Fuckers. I hated my passport. In fact, this whole visa business is such a bane that we Indians practically go into shock from the excitement of discovering that we can freely barge in and out of Singapore. *Let's go to Singapore! They give you the visa on arrival—on arrival, can you imagine? Let's all go to Singapore!* Anytime a country allows us entry that doesn't involve a stack of paperwork a mile high, it's news, and Indians start researching all the ways in which we can conceivably have a family vacation in Bhutan. *It's really not that inconvenient to get to!* But there is nothing more fun than being let into a white country without a visa. Which is why most of us still get a hard-on when we discover that our Green Cards allow us to freely enter and leave not just America but Canada as well! *Oh, let's go to Canada. I hear the Niagara Falls look so much prettier from their side.* We also take pleasure in finding countries worse off than us. *Ha! Pakistanis can't travel anywhere—they can't even travel to India. Ha!*

If you are a non-Indian passport holder and you are in a relationship with an Indian passport holder, and your Indian partner has suggested a surprise getaway for the two of you then you should be very flattered because what you should know is that the Indian has spent at least one week assembling the following: passport size photographs in very particular sizes, bank statements to prove solvency, proof of hotel and ticket bookings, a letter from his or her employer assuring the consulate that the person is gainfully employed, has permission to go on holiday and will have a job upon their return, a visa application promising that he or she is not involved with drug cartels, terrorist organizations, smuggling rings, or in the business of prostitution and human trafficking, and, last but not least, is in possession of an insurance policy that will pay for their remains to be shipped home in the event that they drop dead. The message is clear—we don't particularly want you when you are alive and we definitely don't want to have to have anything to do with you once you are dead.

But the visa that causes us the most stress is the American visa. Back in 2000, when I first applied for mine, we were taught to approach the process with the understanding that the consulate officials needed no real reason to deny you entry into the land of opportunity. Yes, it's true you may have all your documents in place BUT if you stood the wrong way or appeared too cocky or anything you could be going home with a big 'REJECT' stamp on your Indian passport, which made the next time you applied for a visa that much more complicated.

Have you been abroad at all?
Yes! I was in London and Greece last year.
Oh! Then you will definitely get a visa.
Really?
Of course. See, you went to a country like England and you didn't try to stay so they will give you a visa.

Three days later, feeling terribly confident about my chances, I would have another conversation.

Have you been abroad at all?
Yes! I was in London and Greece last year.
Oh shit, that may be a problem.
Really?!
Of course. See, you went to a country like England, the Americans hate England.
Are you sure?
Yes, I am (indignant tone), *don't you read the papers* (supercilious bitch)*?*
What about Greece, do they like Greece?

I had no idea what the hell I was going to do. Listen, America! All I want is to be reunited with my sort-of boyfriend. Why is this being made so hard for me? Isn't this the country that gave us *Love Story* and *Out of Africa* and *The Way We Were*? By the way, readers, if you have not watched these films, do so immediately. They are the best romance movies ever made and you will cry bitterly in the end because real love never ends well. Anyway, coming back to me and the visa—how could a country with Hollywood in it treat me like this?

After obsessing about how fucked I was I finally got down to work and started studying for the GRE. There is nothing more painful than being an adult and having to wake up an hour earlier than your hung-over roommate so you can do standardized tests, the results of which confirm everything you already knew about yourself—that you are stupid and have no aptitude for numbers and reasoning. But I persevered and after three months of this pain and aggravation had managed to scrape together a score of 1920 out of 2400 on my GRE, a score I was given to understand was enough for the courses I had planned to apply for.

I then got around to sending out applications to four universities. The basis for the selection of the said universities was 1. Proximity to New York City and 2. Proximity to New York City. Lucky for me, Syracuse University was probably in the process of diversifying its graduate student body and as an Indian female I got admission to a master's programme in Advertising. Presumably my 'international experience' would enhance the classroom discussion—it was a good thing the admissions committee hadn't actually seen me at work. To my extreme surprise, I also received a rather generous waiver of tuition fees and a job as a teaching assistant to one of the course professors. If anyone was more surprised by this windfall than I was it would have been my parents. Until then the only people we knew who received scholarships and whatnot were very bright kids who were ambitious and had shown academic promise all their lives. I had shown absolutely nothing of the sort. Naturally, this led to Syracuse University's credibility being obliquely and not-so-obliquely questioned. But I didn't care. I was in. Well, almost.

I set about carefully assembling all my visa documents, including a letter from my boss lying about my salary, my position with the company and above all what a brilliant future lay ahead of me should I choose to return to India post my degree. Although I did not need this, I also had a letter of invitation from my father's friend who worked at the United Nations. Despite what America may think of the UN, as an uninformed Indian, I thought it would force them to take my mission to their country seriously. Thus, cloaked in lies and deception, I sashayed to the US consulate.

Here is the thing about us Indians—even the least competitive, most meek-looking ones like the feeling of being first. First in class, first in a race, first born, first anything. So being first in line at the consulate office was no exception. Even though the first interview begins at 9 a.m. the queue itself begins to form the previous night. I hear that the consulate has since changed its rules thus doing away with all the queuing and whatnot, but back then you got in line and waited. And as ridiculous as it sounds, at 9.00 a.m., after having been awake most of the night and dehydrating completely, the first person in that queue actually looks victorious. It is utterly idiotic, totally moronic and a complete waste of time. I showed up at 6 a.m. and spent the next few hours being jealous of all the people in front of me.

Even at six in the morning this queue that I was standing in was a hive of entrepreneurial activity. Hawkers were selling everything from bottled water to packaged snacks to full-blown Indian breakfasts complete with disposable utensils and a bus boy who would pour water on your hands after you had finished eating so you could rinse them off. But what most impressed me was the mobile photography unit. The photographer had a Polaroid camera dangling from his neck and was accompanied by his assistant, a child of no more than ten, who carried a dangerously large pair of scissors and a grubby looking white sheet. They looked half-asleep and fully asleep respectively. These two shuffled up and down the queue—the assistant keeping a respectful distance behind his boss—both chanting *ess saar passpitcher ess madam passpitcher* repeatedly until they found someone who had brazenly shown up with no pictures.

As it happened, the man immediately in front of me had no photographs. The photographer told him how much it would cost, took his money and then turned to his sidekick and yelled something at him in Tamil. The sidekick immediately tucked the scissors into his pants, and in one fluid movement unfurled the sheet handing me one corner to hold. He wordlessly communicated that I should hold it up thus creating a screen behind the subject. A few minutes later, the man was in possession of four freshly and crookedly sliced passport pictures.

Finally, at 9 a.m. the gates to my future were flung open and the line began to trickle into the compound. Having paid several visits to the consulate over the previous six months, I felt like I was visiting an old friend and was very confident of what to expect. But, other than the old rule of no gadgets and no bags, I was in for a rude shock. Unlike the laid-back quiet air of my earlier visits, the process for visa application looked like a set-up akin to what the Nazis must have had at one of their less threatening concentration camps.

The first person we applicants encountered once inside the gates was an officious Indian in uniform who checked our documents to make sure they were piled in the correct order. Anyone who dared to have piled things the wrong way was berated, as an irate mother would scold her five-year-old. After being roundly humiliated we were walked to what can only be described as a sort of caged area where we formed a snake-like queue. It was only here that I realized something; I had never until this day seen Indian people form a queue! Never! We are incapable of standing patiently in a line. Waiting our turn is just something that is absent from our DNA. But here we were like sheep, standing benignly, unafraid of someone pushing past us because at last the Americans had taught us how to do this.

The hours seemed to drag past but as the line moved forward, getting us all closer to the interview, the fear of rejection put everyone in a chatty mood and I discovered that there is a sort of caste system for visa applications. At the very top of the food chain is the business visa—they could be viewed as the Brahmins or the priests. They have the backing of a company that will take all responsibility for them and so it is highly unlikely that their application will be rejected. Second in line is the student visa— the Kshatriyas or warrior class. Of course anything could happen in battle but if the warrior keeps his cool and has a scholarship, it was more than likely they would be approved. Of course, there is always a killjoy in the queue.

The visa officials look at the GRE score as well, one such busybody informed me.

Really? That makes no sense.

My cousin had a very low score and that is why he was rejected.

What was his score, I asked, praying it was at least 100 points lower than mine.

I don't remember, but it was low.

What is your score? I asked, knowing just by looking at the bloody git that it was probably way out of my league.

2400, he smiled with false modesty. I wanted to kill him.

Coming back to the caste system: third in line, and trying the hardest are the tourist visas. They are the Vaishyas or traders. No one respects them and they are a long shot. And, finally, at the very bottom of the barrel is the tourist visa applicant who is a single woman. She is an Untouchable. You see, the single Indian female is seen as someone who wants to go to America to marry, and make no further contribution to the great US of A. There was one such lady standing behind me and I could feel her despair grow as Mr Asshole with the 2400 GRE score went on and on about all his fucking cousins who had had their tourist visas rejected.

A few hours later we made it into the actual building. Chairs and air-conditioning at last! We had the option of using the toilets as well but I had got rid of all the water in my body via sweating so I took a number and took my seat. The room we were in was massive and eerily quiet. All the applicants, and there must have been a few hundred in there, sat in rows like an audience facing a stage except we faced a counter of windows and behind each window sat an American. The glass between them and us was bullet proof, it said so on a sticker. I observed each of these people doing their job. Some of them seemed happy and genuinely interested in the people they were interviewing. Some looked much like I did at work—pissed off, bored shitless and just waiting for 6 p.m. when they could go home and watch *Ally McBeal*. I prayed I would get a happy one.

And then they were calling my number. There were two windows open—a man who looked tired and a lady who looked pissed off. I ended up with her. I crept up to her window, petrified and hoping that she would see how deserving a candidate I was. Or that she would feel pity. I would take either. I slid my papers through a little gap. She flipped through them, as I stood there making every effort to appear as subservient as possible. Eventually she looked up and I gave her my winning but not desperate smile. She did not smile back.

Where you going to?

Syracuse University. I probably said this with doubt in my voice as if Syracuse University were a made up name because her next question seemed full of suspicion.

Is that it?

Wait a minute. Was she onto me? Did she somehow know, just by looking at my face, that the real reason I was doing all this was because I wanted to go to America and marry my sweetheart. I was an Untouchable in a Kshatriya's clothing and she was onto me. Telling the truth would probably be best but instead I lied.

Yes. That's it, I managed a casual tone and gave her, despite my fear, some pretty solid eye contact. *And,* I heard myself saying, *I will be visiting my uncle who works at the UN.*

I instantly regretted it. What if she didn't like the UN? What if now was the time the Americans were fighting with the UN? Why the fuck hadn't I read the papers!

I was red with the shame of having tried to impress her with my flimsy UN connections.

Pick your passport up at 3 p.m.

What? I asked stupidly. Not because I couldn't hear her but because I couldn't believe it!

I said, pick your passport at 3 p.m.

This, as we all know, was code for 'you can enter America'. I thanked her three times before backing away from the counter like a supplicant in a royal court whose execution had been stayed. It had taken ten hours of emotional upheaval but now I had in my possession a true blue American Visa. I was on my way.

SO THIS IS THE LAND OF THE FREE

I arrived in Syracuse at the tail end of the summer of 2000. I travelled from New York City on the Greyhound bus service with a stop at Binghamton. There were a lot of students on my bus. I suspected that they were mainly undergrads because they wore shorts, flip-flops (aka bathroom chappals) and were all wired to some device or other. In other words they looked young. I looked old. I was wearing full-coverage clothing in an effort to protect myself form the air-conditioning that is always working overtime on any from of transport in the western world. I had once boarded a flight in a rather cavalier manner wearing a sundress and sandals. I was miserable the whole journey and have since, regardless of the time of year, travelled with the following items packed in my carry-on: socks, long sleeved top/shirt/thin cardigan, and a light shawl or blanket, thus prompting a friend to say that whenever he travelled with me he felt like he was travelling with his grandmother.

Anyway, I didn't care what I looked like at that moment. I was excited, this was the start of my new life. I could not wait to tell someone, anyone, that I was going to 'grad school'. I could not wait to buy myself a sweatshirt with 'SYRACUSE UNIVERSITY' or similar splashed across it, and I could not wait to meet all my future, cool, international friends. I was finally in America!

Unfortunately, the America I was expecting was so strongly based on what I had seen in the movies that I will admit I was a little disappointed by what Syracuse had to offer. Of course, it was stupid of me to have spent a week in New York City prior to my arrival there. New York can make anything and anyone look dull in comparison. The most boring evening in New York is cooler and sexier than the most interesting evening anywhere else on the planet. And moving from there to Syracuse was akin to having sampled the very best Colombian cocaine and then having to settle for your local dealer's diluted chalk powder version—and the first inkling I got of this was at the Syracuse bus terminal.

If small-town Indian bus terminals are just filthy then small-town American bus terminals are just depressing and the antithesis of everything the America of my dreams stood for. This is not entirely the fault of the terminal itself; the fact is that in America the only people who use the long distance bus service are people who can't afford to fly or drive and this includes hobos, winos, other down-on-their-luck types and students. Most of the students had been disgorged at Binghamton and so I was now left with people who essentially looked like they were unemployed, possibly on parole, and bereft of decent dental health insurance. Naturally, I considered myself to be above all of them. I was an educated Indian woman with healthy (if not cosmetically perfect) teeth and I was taking the bus because, yes I was poor now, but as soon as I finished school I would no longer be poor. What separated me from them was that I had a future.

Looking down upon the less fortunate kept me going only until we exited the station when I noticed several of them being met by friends or relatives in cars. I, on the other hand, had to find myself a taxi. *They are right outside the terminal.* Mitali, my only acquaintance in Syracuse had told me this. Mitali was dating a friend of Thaks' and, like an angel of mercy, had told me I could stay with her until her new roommate showed up. This is a very Indian thing and I will always love Mitali and hold a very special place in my heart for her. Her generosity of spirit helped cure my homesickness and gave me two weeks to find a more permanent place to live.

Unfortunately, Mitali may have somewhat exaggerated the proximity of the taxi stand and while it wasn't very far from the bus stop it felt like it was miles away because I had so much luggage. This is the other Indian thing. When leaving our motherland for any length of time we pack like Jews fleeing wartime Poland. It's like we are going away forever and so all Indians own two gigantic suitcases that are reserved for travel abroad. Besides every single piece of clothing I owned, mine were packed with photographs of all my friends, little knick-knacks that I could decorate my room with, and that held sentimental value, and a Hawkins pressure cooker, which is sort of like an American Express card for my people—we don't leave home without it. At that time, I had, at best, a rudimentary knowledge of how to work a pressure cooker but it seemed like the most practical thing to bring along. In addition to the two ridiculous suitcases I had a strolley, a duffle bag and my handbag. As I trudged towards the taxi stand dragging my worldly possessions behind me, I was relieved that international air travel insisted on a baggage limit because who knows what else I would have tried to pack.

There was no line at the cab-stand and so as soon as the first one showed up I got in and gave the man Mitali's address. We drove through downtown Syracuse towards the university. Because it was a Sunday, downtown was completely deserted. I had never seen such empty streets before. Once, when driving from Calicut to Bangalore, I had wanted to pee and so we kept driving in the hope that we would find a slightly deserted patch of highway for me to squat. We never found that spot. There was always a house or a shop or a person herding animals or just taking a stroll. In America I realized I could pee anywhere, in broad daylight, with my modesty intact.

I got to Mitali's place and there, just a few blocks from where she lived, was the university that on first sight appeared to be everything the brochures had promised me it would. The campus was lush, manicured and sprawling. The buildings were a mix of old and new. The Newhouse School—which is where I would spend my year—had a distinctly 70s feel to it and so as a child of the 70s, and a fan of all things disco, I was in heaven. After gazing at what would be the venue for the next year of my life, I began the arduous task of hefting my luggage from the street to the stoop of the building.

Once I had everything placed right outside the security door I rang the bell. I was looking forward to a nice cup of tea which I knew I would be able to enjoy even if Mitali was a coffee drinker because in addition to my pressure cooker I had sensibly brought with me a box containing 500 Lipton teabags. No one answered the door. It was a Sunday and so she could not possibly be at work. Plus, she knew I was arriving today because we had talked on the phone and exchanged emails about it. I hit the buzzer again and then again and then again before finally admitting to myself that she was clearly not in the apartment.

When one has made a big change in one's life quite often the adrenalin from the excitement of all that is new keeps panic at bay. Naturally, if one is an intrepid traveler then a glitch in travel plans means nothing. I, however, was not an intrepid traveler. I hadn't really been anywhere and the few times I had, I took care to bring along an intrepid traveling companion. This was the first time I was this alone and the fact that things were not going according to plan completely freaked me out. First, I conducted a little pity party for myself. Why was this happening to me? I was in a strange place, my boyfriend didn't want to marry me immediately, and I was utterly exhausted from moving my luggage about. This was too much for anyone! And now on top of everything Mitali, my guardian angel, was missing in action.

Once I had got that out of my system, I started to notice something that took me from self-pity to paranoia. Dusk was beginning to fall and like the downtown part of the city, the area near campus was devoid of people. Every now and again a car would drive by but that was it. Not a single soul was on the streets. Now, instead of worrying about how sad my life was, I started to worry about my life itself. The whole place had a very *I Know What You Did Last Summer* sort of vibe to it, the only sound was the rustle of leaves on the trees, a soothing sound I realize but not in the context that I found myself. In fact, the fucking trees only added to my dread. They were plentiful, and while they definitely were great for the environment and general beauty of the place, they cast long, dark shadows in which murderers and rapists could hide. I sat there hoping Mitali would be happy when she finally rolled up to find my decapitated remains on her doorstep when I suddenly noticed a police car had come to a stop in front of the building.

Excuse me, miss? Are you waiting for someone? I am always nervous when addressing or being addressed by police officers. There is a story about Boy George. Apparently, he was high off his tail and in a coke-induced paranoid fit called the cops because he thought someone was trying to break into his home. The cops showed up, found no intruders, and arrested Boy George because of the quantity of coke they found lying on his coffee table. I don't use coke, mainly because of this story, but I always think that this is a version of something that could easily wind up happening to me.

He probably thinks I am a homeless person like the ones at the bus stop, I thought, as I nervously approached the squad car, hoping that my middle-class subservience would convince the man I was not a threat to the neighbourhood. I explained, in unnecessary, guilty-sounding detail, my predicament so he would know I wasn't planning to set up a little shanty against the side of the building.

After listening patiently he asked if I could call my friend.

I was on the verge of telling him that a true friend would not have allowed the situation to dissolve into this mess but instead I answered the question. *No, sir, I don't have a cell phone.* Like an idiot I had decided to forgo a cellular phone because it had seemed like a luxury until this very moment. *Well, I don't have one either,* he unhelpfully informed me. To be honest, I was surprised to hear this. Didn't everyone in America have a cell phone? What sort of cop was he? *I could drive you up to the Ramada to make a phone call if you like.*

This was very kind of him but what was I to do with my luggage? As if reading my mind, he said, *We'll be back in no time, your bags will be safe.* I didn't believe him. In fact, I was convinced that, with my luck, the bags would most certainly be stolen by the time we got back; but on the upside, if they did disappear at least I was with the person who would be forced to help me find them.

I was about to get in front next to him when he told me I had to ride in the back. He then drove me up the street towards campus and into the portico of the Ramada Inn hotel, bringing the car to a halt right in front of the lobby. The lobby was busy and one half of me was thrilled to see so many people there while the other half wasn't so sure. *They won't mind if I call from here, will they?* I thought it was a valid question given that everyone had seen me get out of the back of a squad car like a common criminal. He assured me that they would have no objection whatsoever and so I went inside to use the phone. I tried Mitali's number several times to no response and I finally left a message on her voicemail begging her to please come home and then went back out to the police officer to let him know what was up.

Maybe you can stay at the hotel, he suggested, as he drove me back. I went from being in his debt to thinking he was an over-privileged ass for suggesting an option this ludicrous. I was a student, with no cellular phone, who had arrived on the Greyhound and was to stay in a friend's place because I had no place of my own. What part of this would lead anyone to think I could afford to shack up in a decent quality hotel? Anyhow, he dropped me back and quite sweetly tried to reassure me that he would be patrolling the neighbourhood and that he was sure my friend would turn up soon. A friend who was slipping to acquaintance status. I thanked him, breathed a huge sigh of relief on finding my luggage intact and sat back down on the stoop to wait.

I was just about to start seriously considering where the heck I was to spend the night when out of the gloom stepped Mitali. I was so relieved to see her I didn't care that she had completely forgotten I was arriving and had instead shoved off to the gym. After moving my stuff in we had a cup of tea, and like true girlfriends bonded immediately over the similarity of our respective love lives. We were both dating men we were infatuated with but who were clearly not so infatuated with us. The fact that our boyfriends knew each other made us sisters-in-arms; the fact that we divulged all this information to one another on what was essentially our second meeting ensured that we were sisters.

Mitali let me stay in the second bedroom of her little flat. The room was no more than seven feet wide and about as long but I didn't mind. For one thing, despite the two giant suitcases I didn't really have a lot of stuff and for another it was a temporary arrangement. Her actual roommate, a computer science grad student, would be arriving in two weeks which was when the semester was scheduled to begin. I had to report earlier because of the teaching assistant position I'd managed to secure. The university had thoughtfully prepared a week-long orientation programme for us.

I went to bed anxiously anticipating the next day.

■

The orientation programme for international teaching assistants, or TAs, was definitely a big deal. It was being staged for all TAs across all departments and so there were at least a few hundred of us at this thing and the first day felt exactly like the first day of a new job. I spent way too much time wondering what to wear so that I would look like I had spent no time wondering what to wear, which in the end was what I always wore when having to straddle the delicate line between formal and casual wear—jeans and a button-down black shirt. The top-half takes care of the teaching assistant, grown-up part of me, while the jeans represent the college student, anti-establishment part.

Even though an email from the international student centre had informed me that the first session was to commence at 9 a.m. I arrived thirty minutes ahead of schedule because the email had also informed us that breakfast would be served for an hour starting at 8 a.m. The Americans, I realized, had the right idea—by giving us free food they had guaranteed 100 per cent, on-time attendance. Amongst the many American stereotypes I held dear the 'standard American breakfast' was one of them. My days of working with the Taj hotels had given me the idea that all Americans ate a combination of eggs, some sort of yummy, salty pork product (bacon/ham/sausage/all three), toast and coffee first thing in the morning. I looked forward to this immensely.

As I took my place in the food line I realized that I would be eating quite a different meal entirely. The true American breakfast is designed to induce a caffeine-sugar-shock buzz and so what I had before me was an assortment of highly processed, highly sugared carbohydrates—Danish pastries, bagels, and muffins—which I found out that day were basically giant-size cupcakes with no frosting. The healthy people ate bagels with cream cheese. I went with the Danish because I had never eaten one before and it looked like the most decadent thing there—its buttery, gooey, strawberry-jammed centre luring me in.

An announcement was made requesting us to stop stuffing our

faces and head towards the auditorium. On my way in I had to stop at a desk that was being manned (or in this case womanned) by two perky volunteers. After I gave them my name they handed me a laminated name tag that I could wear around my neck and a canvas tote bag, the contents of which I subjected to a thorough inspection as soon as I took my seat. There was a notebook and pen that we could presumably use to make notes over the next few days, a folder with our health insurance forms that we would be taught more about, another folder with all kinds of information about the university and my favourite item, a ceramic coffee mug with 'International Teaching Assistant Orientation Program' on one side and '2000' on the other.

I gazed at the coffee mug lovingly; if Syracuse University and I were embarking on a new relationship then this mug was our engagement ring. As with the case of an engagement ring, I did not get much use out of it. I wasn't a coffee drinker then, it was too small for the quantity of tea I required to wake up, and if I had to be honest it wasn't my favourite colour and ended up as a pen-stand on my desk. But it was a daily reminder that I belonged, in this case to a group of nerdy international students who in the year 2000 would earn their living in the same way—by training the impressionable minds of America's youth.

As the days went by, people started to make friends. As human beings we gravitated to our own and being an Indian human this wasn't hard to do given that a large proportion of TAs were desi. I made the classic error that some Indians make and decided I would not be bonding with people just because they were Indian. I had come all the way here and planned to get my international exposure on. Befriending Indians was hardly something I planned to do. Mitali was already in my life and I decided this would be enough. But here is what I loathed then but love now about our Indian brothers and sisters—if you lose them, they will still find you, and ask you lots of personal questions.

What is your stipend?

I was being stared down by a nice computer science major from Hyderabad. I gave him the number and watched as unbridled joy spread across his face. He was, he informed me, getting double. Indians are never happy until they find a person they are better off than. I got the feeling I was going to make a lot of people happy.

Then, during one of the lunch hours, I found myself standing on the periphery of a group of Indians. The bulk of the group was made up of TAs and all of us were listening wide-eyed to another Indian tell us about how fucked we would be if we didn't buy a car. I had joined this bunch a little late in the conversation but it was clear from the unquestioning reverence with which everyone was listening to the man that he had established his credentials. He wasn't a newbie like us, he was a PhD student who had obviously been around the Syracuse campus for a while. And he had a car.

If you don't have a car, forget it. You can't even go grocery shopping.

But isn't the store on campus enough? This was from a nervous looking girl who looked like she had sat up most of the night crying. I wasn't homesick, having a lot of experience being away from my family, but it was pretty clear that for some people this was the first time.

Campus store?! PhD guy spat, *have you seen it? There is nothing there.* He was right about that. Unless one planned on a subsistence diet of eggs, Sprite and cigarettes there really wasn't much else. It was an emergency pit stop when one ran out of washing detergent and not really the place you went to buy weekly supplies. The girl looked like she was going to start crying again. I didn't blame her; the look on all our faces was the same—reflecting our collective minds—where the hell were we to get the money to buy and then maintain a fucking car?

Don't worry, I whispered to the girl, *my friend told me we can get the bus to Wegman's.* Wegman's was the nicest supermarket in all of Syracuse. Unfortunately, PhD guy heard this.

First of all, Wegman's is the most expensive market, he said, dismissing my suggestion and also ignoring the fact that it could not possibly be more expensive than having to buy a car. *BJ's and Price Cutter are much cheaper but the bus stop is very far from both.*

My roommate has a car, offered another bystander. I was absolutely sure that Mr Know-It-All wouldn't have a comeback. But I was wrong.

Does he have snow tires? he asked, with a smug expression on his face, at which point I wondered if the PhD guy was moonlighting as a used-car salesman.

■

We passed the days in a variety of workshops designed to teach us how to teach, what to expect with students, how to apply for a social security number, how to open a bank account, and generally how to live in the US of A. We also sat through lectures on American culture, one aspect of which was that no one batted an eyelid when a student brought food into a classroom. Some of the international TAs were 'international' in name only. They had spent their undergraduate years in America and were very much American other than their accent. Early in the programme, Nissa Larapova, who I ended up getting quite friendly with, marched into a presentation of all the health insurance plans available to us, armed with a huge container of coffee and an egg sandwich that she proceeded to enjoy right under the presenter's nose. This would never have happened in an Indian classroom, and the reason it would not have happened is because it would have been considered disrespectful to do anything but give a professor your fullest attention regardless of how boring he was. I loved America.

During this week-long programme, the university had also organized a series of talks on the rules and regulations by which staff members of the university were to be governed. The one that stands out most clearly in my memory was the lecture about sexual harassment. Sexually harassing a student was against the law and the person in charge of this segment of the programme strenuously warned us against this course of action. Clearly he had every reason to be worried that one of us would wield our power in an inappropriate manner, after all, as he warned us, it had happened before.

As I looked around the room at my fellow TAs it occurred to me that we were essentially a nerd fest from hell. Every geek from India, China and then the rest of the world was present, and prior to this seminar I would not have been able to picture a single one of us sexually abusing anyone, much less a strapping American student. But now that it had been mentioned I could picture little else.

■

My main mode of entertainment during this time was TV. I have always been a fan of wasting my time, I have been doing it ever since I was aware of the world around me. TV, therefore, has been a top favourite pastime, or, as we say in India, 'time pass'. The only thing that makes aimlessly staring at a screen even better is if I am also stoned, but I wasn't a stoner when I got to Syracuse so I would watch hours of nonsense completely sober—which when I think about it is even stupider.

I was a particular fan of absolute trash—my favourites were *The Jerry Springer Show* and *Maury*. Both shows focused on people no one would ever admit to knowing, let alone admit to being. There were shows about fourteen and fifteen-year-old girls who were shagging every single thing that moved and cheerfully informing the audience that they never used condoms and didn't care about pregnancy or AIDS. Then there were shows about relatives having sex with one another, women sleeping with their daughters' boyfriends, fathers sleeping with their daughters' boyfriends and various other unsavoury combinations of sleeping partners. These shows were such crap that watching *Oprah* was a huge step up and felt like going to church for confession—it would cleanse me of the garbage I was filling my mind with the rest of the time.

There was a lot of crying, screaming and fighting on these shows, which is why there were actual bodyguards hired to stand on the sound stage and intervene if a son got angry enough at his dad for sleeping with the former's girlfriend. Where, I wondered, were *these* Americans? And then I remembered the Greyhound bus terminal. I was disgusted with myself for watching this tripe but I could not look away. What sort of rubbishy creature was I that watching people who were clearly fucked up rated as entertainment? I have to this day been unable to find an acceptable answer to this question. Thankfully, however, these shows were at an inconvenient time for anyone with a job/life and so I knew that in a few days when the semester began this would all end. I was like an addict bingeing out before going cold turkey.

The other activity I had started up was exercise, the only decent habit I have managed to cultivate over the years. I was fairly young when I made the connection between exercise and self-esteem and so no matter what else may be going down I know that I can get some measure of peace if I go run or lift or stretch with intention. In 2000 I was still a runner. I wasn't a great runner—my form was probably painful to watch—but I gave myself an A for effort because I got out there almost every morning and clocked between five and eight kilometres, sometimes all the way up to ten. As part of our orientation course we were taken on a recce of the facilities available to us, and the gymnasium was one of them.

Of course, Syracuse University, being well known for its college basketball and football teams, had a separate, elite gym for the athletes, but on seeing the gym the rest of us trolls were allowed to run around in I was so impressed I could not understand what more the athletes would need or want. I adored the gym. It was a huge hall with high ceilings and more equipment than I had ever seen. Until then I had never run indoors on a treadmill and that was the first thing I wanted to try.

The other reason I loved the gym was all the fit people who would show up there. While the semester hadn't commenced for real there were many graduate students who had come in early or may have been there all along working on some paper or other. Many of these men and women were truly fine human specimens and I could watch both the male and female units perform their exercise routines for hours. The only reason I did not was because I didn't want to freak anyone out. But it was amazing—I had never seen such physical beauty or raw power this close. There were women in there that could bench press more weight than the average Indian man! It was wonderful to see these sturdy women do their thing. Then, of course, there were the men. Tall, broad-shouldered, in their tiny little running shorts pulverizing the treadmills. All this meant one thing—I was a gym regular, I looked forward to my one hour there like I was off to a party.

Besides feeling guilty for watching bad TV and feeling holier than thou from my workouts, I was kept busy with the hunt for an apartment. I wasn't fussy, I just wanted clean people to share the bathroom and kitchen with, and I knew I would be sharing because I was looking for the cheapest deal possible. Despite my highhanded plans to find a quirky set of international pals, I ended up finding a place to share with three other Indian women. And here is why—when it comes to our living situation, I found that as an Indian I needed to live with other Indians. You see, we Indians are like vampires. We are so afraid of what our living habits must look like to other people that we form little nests in which we dwell. And so I knew that no matter how crazy these three ladies might prove to be they were known entities. I knew how to deal with crazy Indians and they would know how to deal with me. I could take pictures with foreigners later on. And by 'foreigners' I meant Americans.

We had a weekend between the end of the orientation programme and the start of the semester, and Mitali very kindly drove me, along with my belongings, to the new address. I was no longer as close to campus as I was at Mitali's place, and would have to walk about twenty minutes each way. Mitali assured me that it would be fine even in winter and that I could go grocery shopping when she went. Take that, PhD Boy, I was going to be fine without a set of wheels. When we got to the house none of the other roommates was in. The landlady, however, was waiting for us with a set of keys. She left after making it very clear that it was a non-smoking house. I lied and assured her I had no problem with this rule. Mitali and I then explored the house. It was dilapidated for sure but by far the largest house I had ever lived in. There was a big living room, dining area and kitchen on the ground floor and four bedrooms of varying sizes on the first floor with one shared bathroom.

The house had an attic that was converted into a bedroom—the only room with an attached bathroom. The landlady did say we could choose any room but had mentioned that in the winter the attic tended to take a very long time to heat. Nonetheless I kabza-karoed the attic bathroom—it was tiny but utilitarian and I hoped that my other three roomies would be too lazy to haul ass up a flight of stairs just to pee. The house had a basement, which was about as creepy as a basement can get. It was musty with old furniture and bits of wood lying in corners. It was also dark, the only light source being one naked, low-wattage bulb that dangled tentatively from the ceiling. I was horrified to know that I would not be able to avoid the basement because the washing machine and dryer, two things that make life infinitely better in America, were located down there.

After Mitali left, and as I was putting my clothes away, it

occurred to me that it was all really happening. I walked around my room. It was quite spacious actually, with two huge windows overlooking the street. I have never been a big one for fresh air or anything but I felt obliged to let some into my sunny new room. My window opened onto a gently sloping roof that, if I wanted to, I could climb on to. The day I had come to see the place before agreeing to take it I had walked past several houses similar to this one and on practically each roof I had seen a human being in a swimsuit, sunbathing. What a bunch of jokers these foreigners are, I had thought.

I finished settling in and was congratulating myself on how amazing it was that I was living in a house that I was paying for myself! I had lived on my own before, of course, but always in apartments; this was a house and something about that made me feel grown-up, a feeling that lasted until the first roommate showed up and my mind went back to sixth grade when I had just joined boarding school and wanted everyone to like me.

My new roommates were equally nervous—well, all of us except Namrata. She was an old hand. She had lived in the house for a year and hers was actually the only room that was already taken when I got there. This was her last semester as a computer science major after which she would take up a job in California that she had closed over the summer and that paid her $75,000 a year. Because I was aware that, as a media studies major, once I graduated I would make subsistence wage at best, I immediately judged Namrata as a smug overachiever but graciously congratulated her on her achievments.

The next one to arrive was Damini, a good Tamilian Brahmin girl. She weighed no more than 41 kg, was high-strung, and had completed an undergraduate program at IIT, Chennai, before getting to Syracuse on a full scholarship to complete a PhD in something clever. She was curious about how much stipend I was getting and, as expected, was pleased to hear that it was substantially less than hers.

I won't lie; I was getting a little annoyed with this blatant competitiveness. It was silly and childish and it was sucking me in. First, I had tried to remain above it, but because I wasn't actually above it this didn't last long. I then tried to pretend I didn't need the money, fronting like I had money already and that this TA thing was just time-pass. But that didn't work either, mainly because it is a well-worn fact that no Indian takes a job, least of all on a college campus, unless they need the money. And so, I finally gave in to how I really felt—which was a quiet, seething, jealous rage. I wanted to hurt the people who were making more money, more specifically, the *Indians* who were making more money. But my ego did not permit me to go public with this information, and so I was forced to feign admiration for her as well.

Once she was done gloating, Damini informed me that she was a pure vegetarian.

I hope that no one will cook meat in the kitchen, she said sweetly.

Well, I replied feeling a little victory coming along, *I am actually almost a pure non-vegetarian, so yes I will be cooking meat in the kitchen.* Her panic more than made up for the fact that both she and Namrata had outdone me on the financial scale.

Will you be storing it in the fridge? she asked nervously.

Yes, I smiled apologetically, *that sort of is what one has to do with meat. But don't worry it won't be everyday. Oh—except for eggs, those I will cook every day.*

And with that I turned on my petty, size-8 heel and marched off to my bedroom thinking that I was definitely going straight to hell but oh how good that had felt.

Later that evening, I got to meet my fourth and final roomie, Shefali. Two things made me like her immediately, the fact that her first fucking question wasn't about how much my goddamn stipend was, but instead: *So we can't smoke in here, is it?* Like me, Shefali also lit up 'once in a while'. When one is far from home, with no money, and smug, well-off roomies, sometimes an illicit fag can make all the difference between temporary happiness and slashing your wrists. Shefali and I had more in common. She and I were both doing graduate programmes at the media studies school, which meant we were in the same miserable income bracket, and we were closer to thirty than twenty which, in the Indian computer science context, meant one thing—we were not virgins and the other two were.

Women bond for many different reasons, and a shared worldview on all things related to sex is one of them. Shefali and I spent many evenings huddled on her balcony—hers was the only room that had one—smoking and bitching about our love lives, past and present. By the end of the first month in Syracuse Shefali had met a guy and was in need of my counsel.

I absolutely will have sex with him, she assured me, *I just don't want to on the first date.*

Why? I thought you liked him. I have never been a believer of the 'no sex on the first date' line of thinking, mainly because I am afraid that the guy may change his mind and it's best to get what one can when one can. Shefali, on the other hand, was a far more confident woman.

I do like him. A lot. That's why I just think I should wait.

Then wait.

But what if I can't?!

That's easy, I crowed, *just don't shave your legs.* Hairy legs, amongst other hirsute body parts, had led to my not having one-night stands for ages. If there is one thing I have learnt from my own experiences it is that self-control is not enough. Women like Shefali and I usually know, on first sight, whether or not we will sleep with a person. There are only two things that can change the course of this decision. The first is if the person in question is uninterested, and the second is if we are growing out the hair on our legs for next month's waxing appointment.

Shefali was impressed with my idea. *I never thought of that,* she said, and then left me to go take a shower and get ready for her no-sex first date. Twenty minutes later, she was back looking slightly guilty.

I shaved my legs.
Even your thighs?
Even the thighs, she sighed.
Whore, I smiled, and went back to my book.

WHITE PEOPLE WEATHER

There is an old joke about how when you have nothing to say to someone you talk about the weather. I am not sure who made that one up but they sure as hell did not come from Syracuse. If you have ever spent any time in Syracuse then talking about the weather is a perfectly acceptable way to make conversation. To begin with they actually have four seasons. And the first one I experienced was fall.

Fall is the American name for autumn and what we call 'the rest of summer'. *You have simply GOT to see New England in the fall!,* a friend said to me. She, like most people, was enthralled by the poetic change of colours during this season, whereas I was completely taken up with the fact that every single leaf on every single tree had, quite literally, fallen off. I had never seen so many trees denuded en masse. The last time I was surrounded by this much foliage was in boarding school but those were eucalyptus trees and they were leafy all year round. I know there is a word for all-year-round-leafy-trees but I am too lazy to look it up on Google. Ok, I looked it up—they are called 'evergreen'. Anyway, the point is, I had never seen this phenomenon and was quite intrigued by it.

Everything in Syracuse is dictated by the season or, at the very least, food and fashion most certainly were. If you go into a Starbucks, for instance, you will find them shilling a most delicious concoction called a Pumpkin Spice Latte. This is a seasonal specialty and something that several of my American friends actually sit around in anticipation of all summer long. Of course I only watched and admired Starbucks from afar; I was busy using my imported Indian teabags to make a far less satisfying, completely free, warm beverage.

The other area that seemed to be seriously impacted by the changing climate was fashion and I learnt all about this by indulging myself in America's favourite hobby—the mall-crawl. The Carousel Mall was something of a Syracuse landmark. At the time, it was one of the largest malls in the United States, which is saying a lot given that malls are quite often the main attraction in most towns. My idea of a night out was to take the bus (damn you, PhD guy) to the mall, walk around the shops, watch a movie, eat at the food court, and then come back home. If Mitali was free she would bring a touch of glamour to the proceedings by driving us there in her car.

Being fresh off the boat I was terribly impressed with the array of shops. It was nuts! I wanted a white button-down shirt and every single store in there sold a version of it. Or home decor! I didn't have any immediate need for an 82-piece dinner set but this did not prevent me from stressing out about which one I would eventually buy when I did throw elaborate, imaginary dinner parties in my elaborate, imaginary New York City loft. As soon as I entered the mall I went into a trance and it took all my willpower, and the most acute middle-class fear of debt, to not buy *something* every time I went in there.

The first time I was actually called upon to buy an item of value was when I figured out exactly how cold Syracuse was going to get over the winter. It was only October so we were still very much within the boundaries of autumn and nowhere close to Starbucks' Gingerbread Latte season but it was already quite chilly by my standards. The Americans were still parading about campus in shorts and T-shirts but I knew I was going to have to buy protective clothing sooner than later or risk frostbite.

While researching what coat to buy I made the first of many shopping blunders—I took advice from my Indian connections. Please never ever do this. When it comes to winter clothing and where to purchase it, go ask a local, because having lived in nothing but 45ºC we Indians have no concept of cold weather fashion which is why I was influenced to think of winter clothing as merely functional. Colour, cut and fabric were minor details to be ignored completely. Fashion would just let in the cold. To avoid instant death by hypothermia I was told to buy a coat that would accommodate multiple layers of cardigans underneath it. I would also need a pair of gloves, a hat and boots. Once again, style was a non-factor. *What's important is that all your stuff be wind and waterproof. It's your only hope.* This advice came from a fellow Indian who like PhD guy had been in Syracuse forever and therefore had tremendous street cred.

To acquire all of this at a fair price I was directed to the Mecca for every middle-class Indian: Burlington Coat Factory. This is not actually a coat factory although the name conjured up a rather romantic vision of old, bespectacled men in braces tirelessly sewing high quality garments that would protect one from a Siberian style winter. No, Burlington Coat Factory is a discount store that sold every single type of clothing item you could think of, at what I was assured were the best possible prices. The main reason for all the excitement over it was that Burlington Coat Factory had a reputation for carrying brand names, a little out of date, of course, but *as if you care*—was how Supriya, a newbie like me, who had just shopped there, explained away the outdated styles that I would be making my selection from. Purely because she was trying to save me money and in all likelihood meant well, I allowed that mildly insulting comment to slide.

Looking at my final purchases one would completely agree with Supriya's estimate of my need to look trendy. First, let me tell you about my skiing jacket—a hideous, shapeless beige thing, purchased because I believed that beige goes with everything. Except, I later discovered, skin tone. Maybe I would learn to ski, it seemed like it could be fun, and never mind that this thing was so ugly—if it kept skiers who flew down slopes in sub-zero temperatures warm then I was in clover. My hat, gloves and muffler were gleaned from an assortment of discount bins that I found littered about the store. Like my skiing jacket these items were noticeably unattractive. In fact, my gloves, I later realized, were for men, they were too big for me thus making my hands look larger than they really were, adding to my slightly transgender appearance.

Anyway, I was now prepared for winter and not a moment too soon. Literally days from my purchase I awoke to my first snowfall. I put on every single warm thing I had and stalked out into the cold. I enjoyed the sight of the snow and the crunch it made under my new boots. I sent e-mails extolling its beauty to my mother. The next day was the same—and the next and the next. It would not stop snowing. By January I hated the snow, had an acute Vitamin D deficiency and was mildly depressed. I recalled the foreigners lying about in the sun and now I understood why. I could not wait for summer, I was miserable. All of my Indian warmth and goodwill had been frozen solid. I felt like shit and, thanks to the bad shopping advice I had been getting, I also looked like shit. All I wanted was to get the hell out of Syracuse without either dying in a blizzard or fornicating with a freshman.

LIVING THE DREAM

Being unemployed in America is expensive and, in my case, beyond a point it could also be grounds for deportation. My student visa had an expiry date and as a foreigner I needed a work permit to remain in the country, and for that I needed work.

My first job interview was with J. Walter Thompson, the biggest big daddy of advertising agencies. I was thrilled to bits and something in my bones (laziness most likely) told me I would get this, which is why the only preparations I made for this interview was to iron my 'interview clothes'—all newly purchased at the Carousel Mall. The next morning I took the subway down to the JWT offices, or my future workplace as I had come to think of it. Upon exiting my stop I did something I had not done until that moment—I purchased a cup of tea from a street vendor. I felt both magnanimous and successful as I handed over a dollar—now that I was a New York ad executive I would be able to afford for someone else to make my morning bevy. I then strutted *Saturday Night Fever* style down the last few blocks. I was a bit annoyed when I got there because laid out and free for the taking was an array of breakfast items including a variety of high end teabags. I tried not to think about my wasted dollar.

The first half of the day was spent with several members of the Human Resources department. These interviews went swimmingly and by the time we broke for lunch I was feeling pretty full of myself. This feeling of fullness continued as I stuffed myself with delicious pasta followed by ice cream after which I found myself on the fortieth floor of the building for the final interview of the day. This would be conducted by a big shot in the account servicing department, the man who would make the actual decision to hire.

He had an absolutely gorgeous office with stellar views of the city and a fabulously expensive looking carpet that I commented on. *Oh thank you! I bought that in India actually!* he beamed. We made small talk about his visits to India, the carpet and where in India I was from in relation to said carpet, and then after taking great pains to make me feel like we were friends—something Americans are excellent at—he asked me the first advertising related question I had been asked all day and one that by any standards should have been a mere ice-breaker—*what is your favourite ad?* And you know what? I could not come up with the name of a single goddamn one. I spent what must have been thirty seconds, but felt like thirty hours, looking blankly into the air while going *Ummmmm let's see ahhhhhhhhhhhh wow I can't think of a single one hahahaha how odd ummmmm.*

He graciously put me out of my misery by jumping to the next question but I knew that for all practical purposes that interview was over. I barely managed to get out of there without regurgitating my lunch all over his ethnic rug. I slunk back to Thaks' apartment, hating the thought of having to face someone who already had a job. That evening we went out to celebrate Friday night and my first interview. Obviously, I had not shared the debacle that it had been and so while everyone else celebrated, I drowned my sorrows at O'Flanagan's, a neighbourhood bar. By about 11 p.m. I had completely forgotten how badly I had messed things up and a few hours later I was vomiting on the pavement.

That was the last time I took an interview for granted. Fear will force the most self-absorbed imbecile with a misplaced sense of entitlement to shape up fast and I was definitely scared. Panic-stricken, I put my nose to the grindstone and over fifty interviews and several months later I managed to land my first job in America. I was hired by a media buying company to work in the non-traditional media division.

Non-traditional media is basically advertising space that a consumer would never think of. Catching them unawares appeared to be our motto, and on my first day I was given a folder full of amazing, non-traditional opportunities that were already out there. It seemed that advertisers had left no stone unturned in an effort to get their customers' attention. Messages were plastered everywhere—the door of a toilet cubicle, the floor of a urinal, on toilet paper, on sidewalks, on cars and on people.

I was most impressed with the toilet-centric ideas. One could avoid pretty much anything except taking a shit. Far from thinking of it as intrusive I actually thought we were doing them a favour. If time is money then you could wipe your arse AND consider a newer, better credit card, or a softer, more absorbent sanitary pad. I couldn't wait to share some ideas of my own.

As a lowly assistant, however, I was rarely privy to the important meetings between the VPs in our company and the purveyors of this non-traditional ad space but I can only imagine they discussed relevant things.

For the launch of the small business owners' credit card we recommend 200 urinals and 100 stalls because research has shown that more men than women start their own businesses. We do, however, suggest you focus on just ONE message, either go with the low APR or with the great rewards programme, because based on how long it takes for men to pee they won't have the time to read both.

But women take forever—why can't we do both messages in the women's stalls?

We can do that.

AND—I may just be speaking for myself but often when I pee it takes a while for the flow to get going so I would count that in to my total pissing time—quite honestly for the women I say we slam them with low APR, great rewards AND an extended credit line.

I should have been content to spend my days seeking out ways to ambush my clients' customers but advertising executives are like commitment phobic lovers; we are constantly on the lookout for a new job even while we are at a new job and so within a few months at my new job I had yet another new job. This was a huge step up mainly because the word 'assistant' had been taken out of my title and my new employers were willing to process my Green Card—the holiest of holy grails for any immigrant.

I was particularly chuffed with this last bit. You see I had resigned myself to having to wait the usual eight or ten years before being bestowed a permanent residency—back in the dark ages that I speak of that was standard—but thanks to an accident of fate and some rather creative handiwork on the part of the agency lawyer I would have mine in less than two years. As I sat at my desk with no view I had a most unromantic thought—perhaps this might change 'Thaks' mind about wanting to marry me.

Prior to my first day at the agency I sat about daydreaming about my future. A future filled with wonderful, award-winning work that I would constantly be rewarded for. My clients would be those unbearably hip companies with products that every agency would pitch for but only mine would land. I would then be put in charge, travelling all over the world, whipping up brilliant presentations for high-profile meetings with powerful people while I simultaneously trained for a marathon and barked instructions at my underlings via a satellite phone or whatever phone technology one uses when making a call from a private jet.

Then I actually started working there, and without preamble, my fantasies were decimated. One by one, my dreams were tortured slowly and painfully to death, fingernails and toenails were peeled off, knuckles were broken, and kneecaps powdered. When I joined advertising I had naively thought that it was a haven for creative types, people who were quirky and had a million out-of-the-box ideas—people like me. And while this may have been true for my co-workers, in the actual creative department, it was not the case for me. I had been brought on as an account executive in the account servicing department.

There were no jet planes—the closest I got to a private plane was when a group of people from my office were flown on the client's aircraft to Aruba for a TV shoot and I happened to sit next to the girl who planned the trip itinerary. There were no high-profile meetings or marathons either and there certainly weren't any underlings because I was the underling. Account servicing is a thankless job at any level and at mine it was the worst. We are a punching bag for the client and, as an added bonus, get smacked about by every other group within the agency as well. The more I considered it, the more I was convinced that our job had been specifically created to provide everyone else with a legal outlet for their professional and personal frustrations. I went into work every day praying that everyone I would have to deal with had gotten laid the previous night.

My main goal was to not get fired until my Green Card materialized and to this end I engaged in what my grandmother would call window-dressing, and my friend and collegue Varun described as the ability to LBDFA. This was just before the advent of LOL and LMAO and ROTFL and had nothing to do with laughing or enjoyment. What it meant was 'Looking Busy while Doing Fuck All' and as an account executive there were a few things I had taken to doing so that I too looked as if I were gainfully occupied.

The first was moving quickly and seemingly with purpose. My colleague Loretta who worked on the same team as I did had a meandering way about her. I liked Loretta and enjoyed her calm, unfrazzled movements around the sixth and seventh floors of our building where we were generally to be found. Unfortunately our boss was permanently annoyed by Loretta's pace. Account executives were expected to be in a rush; we were the movers and shakers of the agency, and quite often we were told we were the face of the agency as well. This face had to move at 150 miles/hour as if being chased by a wild animal, careening around corners knocking people out, preferably laden with sheaves of paper, not idling away our clients' precious time. Walking like you cared about life and limb was frowned upon.

And so I took to hurrying about the office regardless of where I was going. Even if I were on my way to the loo I would march there, head held high, back erect. The expression on my face, or should I say the face of the agency, was one of determination, focus and drive. Of course, I was determined, focused and driven to get to the toilet before I wet my pants. I had a habit, and still do, of holding on until it's unbearable and within the realm of a possible accident, and this was the look I kept on all day long on the off chance that my boss might see me relaxing and get worked up that I wasn't doing my job. Meetings were more of a comfort zone for me; I know most people hate them because they are so boring, but I loved them precisely for that reason. I could conduct my LBDFA activities in peace and quiet rather than actively buzzing around.

But I did have some actual duties, and 'creative sequencing' was one of them. This is the ability to keep a copy of every version of an advertisement from its inception to the way it finally looked after it has gone through the 123rd round of client mangling. This is a job that in every other industry is simply referred to as filing. Despite my snootiness about it now I will say that the precision of this particular task should not be understated. A good account executive who maintains a solid file of iterations will find use for it when, for instance, the idiot client changes his mind for the eighty-seventh time, back to an idea that you had suggested in round four. That is when you can whip out the evidence and shove it in their face. This has to be done very cleverly though, like you are just looking through your papers and happened to, completely unintentionally, come upon the proof of his stupidity and your brilliance. You can never let it look like you want to make them feel small, as that will only result in them hating you and making your life even more unbearable.

Which is why I was always convinced that no matter what anyone said, the client-agency relationship had nothing to do with teamwork. It was not an alliance based on mutual need; we needed them and, above all else, their money. Which is why they treated us poorly, abusing us at every turn, and we had to lump it, getting back at them in that passive-aggressive way endemic to all dysfunctional marriages. My stand against the client was to not own a mobile phone. That they could not speed dial me every single time they had their underwear scrunched up bothered them no end. Because the agency did not provide a low-life like me with a mobile phone all I could do when asked for my number was smile and shrug my shoulders apologetically. Many of my colleagues had personal phones that they paid for themselves yet gave the number to the clients. These people were not my friends. They were smart and ambitious and I wished to have nothing to do with that type of thing.

My own client was a major commercial bank—let's call them Titty Wank—and I was assigned to what was called the direct marketing operations. I helped create and produce the letters that consumers get every day in their mailboxes—99 per cent of which undoubtedly end up in the rubbish bin unopened. Within Titty Wank the people I usually worked with were part of the marketing department. These harbingers of modern marketing techniques were usually handpicked by their bosses from the leading business schools around the country. Now I have nothing against business schools, I attended one myself. Granted, it was not the leading school on its street, let alone the country, but the fact is that we all had a similar syllabus and marketing majors usually end up taking ONE course in advertising. This wealth of knowledge, in conjunction with the fact that they were my client, gave them the unalienable right to lord it over me, rip all my advertising copy to pieces, tell me to fuck off, and in general make my life insufferably dull.

It was infuriating to watch them luxuriate in abysmal ignorance about practically everything, yet merrily and without good reason tell you that the work sucked. When pressed for some explanation as to what it was that was bothering them, the stock response was *Oh, I don't know, I guess I just don't like it.* Based on that I would have to go back to my team, and have them change everything since we didn't know which part was the problem. I hated my clients and looked forward to our meetings the way one looks forward to a case of haemorrhoids.

The other part of my job was scheduling, an activity conducted primarily within the agency. It involved kissing my remaining shred of self-respect goodbye as I went from one grouchy art director or creative writer to another begging them to remember that the presentation deadline was in twenty-four hours. Now while this task was simple in theory, it was extremely difficult to put into practice because the creative team hated the account team possibly more than the account team hated the client. The relationship between creative and account is almost identical to that of the Shias and Sunnis of Iraq. We wanted the other ones dead on average of about seven times a day.

Oddly enough, I could handle this part of the job and I attribute this to the fact that secretly I wanted to be a creative person. And why wouldn't I? They looked like they were having infinitely more fun than I was. I would have given anything to parade into work at 10.30 in the morning covered in immunity, take long lunch breaks without having to make up any excuse for it, and, as the icing on the cake, be supercilious around anyone who wasn't creative. Plus, as a natural born slob, the idea of never having to comb my hair, wash my face or wear a fucking suit was very appealing. If you see a group of people sitting about an agency in a listless sort of fashion, doing absolutely nothing but staring off into space, I can assure you that they are the creative team and that they are hard at work IDEATING. 'Ideating' is what they put on their time sheets to describe what the rest of us would simply explain as a hangover.

I appreciated that despite working for a corporate company they were allowing a little anti-establishment sentiment to flower. Of course, as an account executive I represented the establishment and so it was a prickly relationship but, eventually, I won them over—I was relentless with my flattery that all creative people will admit is hard to resist and with my constant bitching about the client and all the other account people. Most of the creative team wasn't even that hard to crack. Except for Larry Pierce.

Larry was a senior art director. He looked like what I thought a Nazi youth must have looked like except that Larry was fifty. He was blonder than anyone I had ever seen, his features were razor sharp and he had the sinewy, muscular physique of a devoted gym bunny. When Larry Pierce wore shorts to work I would sit around wishing he wasn't gay. Larry Pierce hated all account people equally and his office was frigid with the hostility that he radiated from every pore.

The first time I encountered Larry it was for a layout of an envelope that would carry an extended credit line to credit card members who we suspected were desperate to take their families on vacation but hadn't the funds at hand. Larry had designed something that involved a photograph of a beautiful beach in the background and the happy feet of a family in the foreground. The client, an inarticulate cow, had hated it stating *Feet freak me out* as her reason. And now I was the one sent to let Larry know this—and if I survived that I would have to get him to provide me with an alternative idea. What made all of this a bit of a minefield was that I was pushed on to the project because the executive-in-charge had quit rather suddenly.

I gingerly tapped on Larry's door and when he swivelled around from his computer screen to face me, the look on his face suggested that if he had a gun it would have been loaded and levelled at the spot between my eyes.

May I come in? I smiled sweetly, hoping that my minority status as a woman of colour would help my cause.

What do you want? he asked, cocking the imaginary gun.

I'm Radhika, I am an account...

Where is Selina? I work with Selina.

I was itching to tell him Selina had quit, in all likelihood due to people like him, but I knew on what side my bread was being buttered so I just explained that she was indeed moving on and that I, poor hapless me, had been sent in to fill her shoes.

Upon hearing all of this, Larry turned back to his computer screen.

I am eating my lunch, you will have to come back after I am done.

Indeed it was close to 1 p.m., the standard time for lunch, but meal times were a rather fluid concept at the agency, plus where was this lunch? Larry's desk was devoid of any kind of eatable save for one shiny red apple. A perfect apple, actually, it looked crunchy and like it had none of those gross soggy surprises lurking within. Frankly, it looked just like Larry Pierce—hard bodied and healthy. I kept staring at the apple, my eyes asking the question my mouth wouldn't have dared; which was *How fucking slowly do you plan to eat that apple?* As if reading my mind, Larry asked me to be back in an hour.

For all my venom and fury, when it comes to actual human interaction I am non-confrontational and actually quite hesitant to be a bitch to anyone's face—preferring instead to hating them behind their backs. For this reason I worshipped Larry, he was always in a bad mood and was never afraid to show it. After a few contentious months we became friends. We hated all the same people and so I would sometimes just skulk around his office long after my work was done so I could watch him torment some other twit that I would never in my wildest dreams either have had the courage or opportunity to humiliate.

And while I was able to deal with the Larry Pierces of the agency, I was never able to crack the bosses. I have never gotten along badly with a boss, I have never had one make my life miserable—although I have seen it done to others—but I always knew that I wasn't going to be the one the boss would fight for. If there was to be a round of redundancies and my name came up, I would be gone. I didn't hold any of this against them because I knew deep down I wasn't their best employee. What annoyed me about them, though, was that whenever they spoke of our work they would insist on using terminology used by army generals, while sitting in an office on 39th Street and Lex.

Let's meet in the war room (a conference room that had been decked out with all the work the competition was doing). *I have a report on the new attack* (ad campaign) *launched by Jamaican Express. As we can see, they have extensive air cover* (TV and radio)—*and they have their men on the ground too* (print media). *How are we going to respond to this? We need to call in the big guns, we need to fight fire with fire, we need to win this battle* (we need to stop goofing off and show the client we know what the fuck we are doing).

With the benefit of hindsight, I will say that we were indeed at war. Maybe not a bloody war but certainly a stressful one. New York is known for many things, and a cut-throat advertising industry is most certainly one of them. Nobody has the time for slackers and purposeless drifters. The very fact that I survived as long as I did was quite a surprise to myself and everyone who knew me; that my career was lacklustre, wasn't. Not all of us can or will rise up the corporate ladder. Some of us will go on to bigger and better things—become directors and VPs and CEOs and whatnot. The rest of us muddle along, never get a promotion or raise and then eventually try our hand at comedy.

WHO WILL MARRY THIS COW?

I'm not living with anyone unless we are getting married. This was Rebecca, my supervisor at work. *I tried it once—moving out was brutal.*

The reason we were having this conversation was because Thaks and I had just moved into our first apartment together and I was having major buyer's remorse. Indians, as a rule, do not endorse a man and woman living together outside the bonds of matrimony. It is the type of lifestyle we refer to as bohemian, to be indulged in by artists and rich people. It is not a stable environment and stability is the cornerstone of a yuppie existence, a lifestyle after which I hankered. I had my reservations too but they evaporated like smoke the moment I found out what it would cost to live on my own in New York City.

But, Becca, anything can end—it's the same as a marriage ending.

No, it's not, she sniggered. *Living together without a plan is like standing still, so when you break up you have nothing to show for it, nothing! Time has passed but nothing of value has been built.*

Rebecca was beginning to sound like a high school Economics professor after her third glass of wine.

Later that week I visited Pier1 Imports where I purchased plates, mugs and Christmas-themed oven gloves for all the cakes I would never bake, and what should have been a fun task was turned in to a chore that I resented because all I could think about was Rebecca's conviction. By the time I got home I had worked myself up into a state of indignation so intense I couldn't wait to start a fight.

My friend Becca says it's weird that we aren't engaged. Classic opener fired off of someone else's shoulder.

I don't really want to talk about this. His standard response.

Why not?

I don't believe in marriage. This wasn't new either. I don't recall the exact sequence of events but it would have ended with one of us crying and the other one taking off for a ten-mile run. No prizes for guessing who did what.

Thus far my time in America had been focused on dealing with practical matters such as the paucity of funds and the constant fear that I would not find a job and have to go back to India. Real life problems had pushed my love life problems to the backburner. But now that I was gainfully employed, and my company was even getting me a Green Card, I had plenty of time to dwell on the tribulations my romance was causing me. In order for me to fully realize this luxury I called Sonali Roy who now lived in San Jose.

So has he said anything? Having enough background on my situation, Sonali did not beat around the bush.

Nothing! I hissed. *Absolutely nothing has bloody changed.* I had to keep my voice down because our one-bedroom place had paper-thin walls and, as every girl knows, when you are dealing with the delicate situation of trying to push and prod a relationship forward, discretion is imperative.

Then you have to do something about it.

I wondered about all those girls who didn't have to plot and plan to get their boyfriends to propose. I hated those bitches and idly wondered about entrapment. Maybe I could get pregnant, that would certainly do it. Yuck. What was wrong with me? I was a low-life to even think this. Or was I?

Hello?

Yes, yes, I am here.

And?

It's just that this is so embarrassing.

Wouldn't you prefer to be embarrassed now and know where you stand? You need to know that way you can protect yourself.

Protect myself! I was a girl who had a hard time asking a guy to slip a condom on. In fact the more I thought about it the more surprised I was that I hadn't already had a mishap. Holy shit, maybe I couldn't get pregnant at all. This thought was a terrible setback to my secret pregnancy plan. On another note, if I couldn't get preggers then all this panic of the last many years over my period being late etc. had been completely pointless and had only served to age me.

What do you mean protect myself? From what?

From getting too involved.

I have never understood this whole 'don't get too involved' business. It reminded me of 'play hard to get', great advice in general but somehow the only time you ever hear it is when you are well past the point of no return. I've always admired people who could do it though. Not me. I wanted instant gratification; my modus operandi was to go all in, all the time, leaving absolutely nothing for later. I was the kid who ate up her share of chocolate only to be left staring at the kid who had smartly saved a little bit as a post-play treat.

Okay, but how do I bring this up without using the word 'marriage'? This was critical. In addition to 'marriage', I was also hoping to also avoid terminology like 'relationship', 'long-term', 'commitment' or 'future'.

Vaz, you just have to be honest about how you feel.

Once again, excellent advice in general. Honesty after all is the basis of any successful relationship, there isn't a self-help book in the history of self-help books that says otherwise. The problem with honesty though is that you have to be a very strong person to stomach the consequences. Weak people like myself tended to be liars and, even worse, preferred to be lied to. Despite Sonali's pep talk I knew I would do diddly squat.

After we hung up I sat there feeling irritated with myself. Was I leaving things as they were because I was so frozen by the fear of being alone or was it because I was deeply in love? Emotions are so hard to separate, although you would think 'love' and 'fear' would be easy enough to tell apart.

We continued to live together as man and something. Our good times in the city that never sleeps interrupted only occasionally when Rebecca or Sonali pointed out that I wasn't getting what I really wanted. Then, one fine night, we were at a party in our neighborhood, and I wound up talking to another guest. She was Indian but born and raised in America and so her name was Melanie, and like so many people who are originally from the Third World but who don't actually have to live here she loved India and couldn't wait to tell me how much.

Oh, my God, I go to India all the time. My dad's from Chennai and my mom's from Mumbai. Non-residents always refer to Indian cities by their politically correct new names that for some reason really bugs me. *I am totally into it, I have cousins there and everything. And I love Shah Rukh Khan.* The mascot of all things Indian.

So where do you live? she asked.

Here in Battery Park.

I'm sorry? she asked the question like she was hard of hearing when in fact it was my Indian accent she was having trouble with.

Battery Park, I patiently repeated, while thinking if your fricking dad is from Chennai how come you have so much difficulty with what I'm saying?

Ohh Battery Park, she repeated in her Valley Girl squawk.

Yes.

Where exactly?

Actually, I said, pointing at the building right across the street—*right there.*

Oh really—that's so weird, that guy over there said he lived there too.

'That guy' happened to be Thaks who at that moment was excitedly pointing our building out to someone else.

Oh yes him—we live together actually, I was smiling at her but my tone was suddenly territorial.

When a woman gets jealous of just about any other woman who comes in any kind of contact with her man it is a universally acknowledged low point. It's not a cute look and is most often directed at women who could not possibly care less about your guy. But it's a feral response and one we rarely have control over.

So, she smiled back, not missing a damn thing, *are you married?*

If I had been in a Hollywood movie, *Gone Girl* specifically, Thaks would have chosen that exact moment to propose to me. With that possibility far out of range I briefly considered lying but decided it was too risky. I knew that she knew that I knew that she knew the truth; she could see my fingers, unfettered as they were by a wedding ring. But instead of giving her a calm, monosyllabic response I overplayed it, thus tingeing my previously territorial tone with defensiveness.

No! I laughed a little too hard, *not at all—we are not married.* Of course, I am hoping against all odds that I have made it clear that our living together is my decision, that it's all up to me, that I choose, and that I have chosen to not be married, because marriage is some bullshit, passé, bourgeoisie nonsense. But of course she knows I am full of it, and now I can feel waves of judgment coming off this girl.

Don't mind if I tell you something, she says, words that always preface a statement that one is most certainly going to mind, *but my dad always says why buy the cow when you can get the milk for free.*

I think I might have strangled her if I wasn't so busy having a conniption. By quoting her Dad From Chennai she was basically calling me a whore. A whore! And not just any whore but one that wasn't even being paid, a whore that doled out credit, a low quality hooker. I had to stand there and listen to how I was giving away my milk—just squirting and splashing it about—all for nothing in return.

A comment like this would have been offensive coming from anyone but as I stood there I realized that if Rebecca had said any of this I wouldn't have cared. With her it would have at best been food for thought and at worst a realization of some sort of truth. But somehow hearing it from one of my own people was borderline traumatic. She had context on me, she knew I wanted to get married and that I was only cohabitating with my man because I hoped it would lead to that, that I was fronting as this cool chick who didn't play by the rules but that all the while I was self-flagellating and self-hating. I may have been living in New York but I was still bound by the rules of my people, I wanted their approval and with my current set-up I would not be having any of it. I was a stupid cow, and she was simply pointing it out. I spent the rest of the evening close to the vodka bottle.

I wish I could say that this experience drove me to higher ground and that I learnt how insignificant this whole marriage act was. I wish I could tell you that this was the moment that I discovered I was worth it, whether or not I had a ring on my finger. Of course, nothing of the sort happened and I ended the evening the way I ended all Saturday nights—drunk.

The next morning, hung-over and ashamed, I awoke to a new day. As I sat there gingerly sipping my tea, beating myself up and replaying the events of the previous night I suddenly realized exactly what my reason for wanting to get married was. I didn't want a ring because I needed to know that all that spilt milk was worthwhile; I didn't even want a ring as proof that he loved me. No, I wanted a ring simply so that other people would think he did.

IV

Marriage and its Aftermath

Two happy, smiling idiots.

CITY HALL

The only people who don't care about money are the people who have it. As an immigrant in New York I felt the same way about the Green Card. I always noticed that the only immigrants with a cavalier attitude towards permanent residency were the people to whom it came easy. If you married a Green Card holder, or even better an American citizen, then you had no idea of the pain and struggle involved, something many of us were reminded of every time we were at a party thrown by one of our fresh-off-the-boat cousins.

When I first got there I was on a student visa. This was like being Cinderella at the ball. You were allowed to party hard but at some point very soon you were going to have to leave or turn into a pumpkin. Being fully aware of my lowly status I would simply stand around listening intently to my more experienced colleagues discuss the ins and outs of becoming a legal alien.

Are you on a Green Card?
Yes. And you?
No, H1B visa.

An H1B visa was a conversation stopper. No one looks up to that except your relatives back home who don't know better. I couldn't believe the guy had even brought up the topic given the side of the fence he was standing on.

But, but, but...my company is applying for my Green Card.
Okay a little desperate but certainly back in the game.
Really? And how long did they tell you it would take?

Oh, you know, the standard five to six years.

Ouch. One of the things you never want to be is the 'standard' guy. Especially not when surrounded by a bunch of smug bankers all of whom have managed to find some loophole that circumvents regular procedure.

Wow—that's a long time to wait. Said with the right amount of sympathy and mystery, this statement will no doubt elicit the next question.

Why? How long will yours take?

A smidge on the defensive side and exactly what we have been waiting for.

Oh, I already have mine. It was crazy—I got in on some 'genius quota' if you can believe that. The false modesty and unnecessary air-quotes are easy to see through. This dude is bragging like he has the biggest dick in the room. And sadly, to the rest of us visa holders, it feels like he does. We are struck by envy and admiration in equal measure.

The reason that this is all such a big deal is because there is one belief that all Green Card applicants subscribe to. We actually think that it will, in some way, shape or form, change our lives for the better. We speak about it rationally enough *I can't wait to have the freedom to quit this shitty job and find something better.* Or *At least if I lose my shitty job now I won't have to leave the country,* etc.

But in our hearts we think that the Green Card is a magic wand. The end to all our problems including those that have nothing to do with being an immigrant. But the truth is that getting a Green Card is like losing your virginity—nothing really changes but at least now when you and your homies get together you don't feel like a tool.

A few years later I had moved myself up the ladder to an H1B visa and like everyone else I had petitioned my employer to put in an application for my Green Card. Because I worked in a job that was hellbent on paying the least amount of money they could legally get away with, I did not expect anything but standard procedure and so I decided that for the next six years at least I would be a model employee. Then one fine morning I got a call from Suzanne, the HR lady.

I may have some good news.

Unless it was a raise we had nothing to discuss.

It's about your Green Card.

Now she had my undivided attention.

Our lawyer, very creative guy, by the way, has found a loophole.

I won't go into the boring detail of all the lovely legal ambiguities of my case. Suffice it to say my lawyer had managed to find the next best thing to "genius quota" and I would be getting the Green Card in less than eighteen months. Shamefully, the first thing I thought of was how dramatically this was going to impact Thaks' vision of marriage given that his own Green Card application was on the standard track—if this thing was a magic wand this would certainly test its ability. And the second thing I thought of was the FOB parties and how I was going to be swinging this dick of mine around anytime anyone so much as thought about the colour green.

I won't say that Thaks married me for my Green Card but about a year from Suzanne's good news I found myself outside City Hall. This was my production. I had liaised with my lawyer on Thaks' behalf, submitted all the paperwork to the City Clerk's office, and because the city has an interesting rule—you have to get a licence at least twenty-four hours before you actually tie the knot thus giving impulsive folk a cooling-off period—I had stood in line two days prior to get my hands on the damn thing. In return my husband-to-be was late. Quite late, in fact, late enough that the security guard who had gruffly informed me she would only let me into the building when 'both parties' were in attendance was now looking at me sympathetically as if I were a poorer and far less glamorous version of Carrie Bradshaw. Please refer to the 'stood-up-at-the-altar' scene from the first SATC movie.

Do you remember anything about that day in City Hall? I once asked Thaks.

Absolutely, Kabir was with us, right? Wasn't he our witness?

Idiot. It was not Kabir but Alix who was with us, and who, in addition to being as late as Thaks, was also seriously hung-over. She had been chosen for two reasons, she was Kabir's girlfriend, and because Kabir had introduced Thaks to me I thought this was a cute idea. But, more importantly, Alix was unemployed at the time and the only person I knew who would be free during working hours. She rolled up looking a little green around the gills, clutching a bagel with cream cheese, a bottle of water and a camera that we eventually discovered did not work. This was a problem because Al was our only witness and those were the days when camera phones were not as rampant as they are now.

Al's camera isn't working, I complained.

That's fine, said Thaks, *what are we going to take pictures of anyway?*

Clearly I was the only one taking any of this seriously.

The three of us joined a long queue of couples and were allowed inside the building only after security had relieved Al of her half-eaten bagel. We wound our way through various corridors until we arrived at the marriage bureau and here we waited with men and women of all ages and ethnicities. Some were dressed for the occasion in suits and wedding dresses.

Good thing Thaks is wearing a suit, whispered Al. *You and I definitely don't look like we belong.*

She was right. Al was wearing whatever she had found on the floor after waking up late and I, while freshly laundered, was wearing jeans and a T-shirt. It was hard to tell which one of us was the bride, a problem the group ahead of us certainly did not have. There was no mistaking who Bridezilla was, she was in a floor-length white gown and veil, and based on the outfits of several others in her party, it was clear that she had two bridesmaids and a flower girl who was weeping bitterly because someone had dropped water on her new bright purple dress.

Before the actual ceremony, there was one final paperwork pit stop at the registrar's office. One couple at a time, we were ushered into a room with multiple windows. Behind each one sat an official. It was the luck of the draw and we got Rhoda. Now I am sure that there is nothing on earth more annoying than to-be-married couples and this sentiment was writ large across her face, She was not amused by any of us, to her we weren't cute, we were just a bunch of self-involved twits who thought, despite standing in line with hundreds of others like us, that we were still special. Rhoda's job was to fill out the information that would eventually end up on our marriage certificate. We went through the usual date of birth, address, etc. and then she asked me, *Will you be changing your name?*. *No*, I replied.

My husband-to-be who had thus far been utterly disinterested in the entire proceedings suddenly came to life. *Wait. Wait. We didn't discuss this.* Rhoda rolled her eyes and gave me a look that said 'Lady, I don't have the time for this shit'. With Rhoda's bad vibes on my side the sheer meaninglessness of changing ones name occurred to me. *Are you planning on changing your name?* I hissed at him. *No,* came his shocked response, like I had asked him to push his mother off a cliff (a request I have since made). *In that case,* I said, *we have nothing to discuss.*

I wasn't resisting a name change due to some deeply held belief about my identity but more because going through with it would be a giant chore. At twenty-five maybe I would have thought the whole business to be a romantic thing, but at thirty-three it was just unnecessary—I wasn't in the mood to run around changing names on my passport and—hullo—my newly-minted Green Card. And if Thaks hadn't had anything to say it would have remained just that, his questioning me about it on the other hand made me think of myself as some new age Betty Friedan.

I didn't change my name, I informed Al on our way to the chapel.

Of course you didn't, said Al.

He wanted me to, I snitched.

Al glared at Thaks, *Why exactly should she?*

I never said she should! No man ever wants to come off as anything but liberal. *All I said was let's just take a minute and weigh the pros and cons.*

Really? asked Al in her best and most sarcastic tone. *And what exactly are these pros?*

The service was non-denominational, quick and painless. And soon we were drinking mimosas with Kabir who had finally fetched up at Bubby's—a very famous brunch place in the heart of Tribeca—one of Manhattan's richest hoods. Normally, the likes of us would have had to wait hours for a table but it was an odd time on a weekday and all the tables were open but one in the far corner.

Rads, Al leaned over to me, *do you know who that is?* She was eyeballing the other table. I looked over and there was seated Mister Nathan Lane, Broadway star, brilliant actor and New York City treasure. While I was slightly more discreet in my gawking, Thaks and Kabir were not and so the four of us spent a few moments openly staring at the man in the same rude way Indian aunties stare at the prettiest girl at a wedding.

Shit, Al! I wish your camera was working, said Thaks. It tells you something that Nathan Lane, an actor he knew practically nothing about, was the highlight of his wedding day.

GETTING READY TO GET MARRIED

In November 2004, I got married for the third time to the same person. First, we went through the aforementioned City Hall deal. Then we had yet another registration at my parents' home in Bangalore—which in hindsight serves no purpose other than to make divorce between us extremely complicated and expensive—and finally we made it to Delhi for the last and final instalment, the Hindu ceremony or, as my mother-in-law likes to call it, 'the actual wedding'.

Regardless of where you are from, every bride knows that the most important decision, bar none, involved with getting married is choosing your bridal outfit. Most women have a good idea of what to wear either because they have strong cultural roots that dictate traditional bridal gear or they are individuals with immense strength of character who don't give a shit about what anyone else thinks and so they go ahead and do their own thing. While I am technically Goan Christian, the last time I saw the inside of a church was when I went into Limelight, an old church that was first converted into a nightclub and then into a shopping mall. Wearing a white gown would have been a surprise to everyone, especially my parents. And so having neither cultural affinity nor the required gumption to pull off something original I began to obsessively troll the Internet hoping to find something to throw on. What did I want to be on my wedding day? Traditional or contemporary? Sexy or conservative? Flashy or low-key? Although, to be honest, I wasn't obsessed with the question of *what would make a statement?* or even *what will make me look fantastic?* While both consequences were welcome, my preoccupation was, quite literally, *what the fuck am I going to wear?*

Sure, I didn't have a clue as to what I wanted but I could start by making a list of all the things I knew were out of the question. And so I did what anyone in my set of circumstances would do: I began the hideous process of growing out my Annie Lennox hairdo. No matter what anyone tells us, the fact is Indian women are long-haired lasses. The percentage of short-haired Indian women who wear their hair cropped as a matter of choice, and not because they are widows or recovering from chemo, is negligible. There is something about long hair that is Indian and feminine and princess-like and on my wedding day I fully intended to embody all three. Six months later, I still didn't have an outfit but I had layers of limp, lacklustre hair that had inched past my earlobes. I was also now the proud owner of a hairbrush, clips, hair bands and a straightening iron. Never mind that I looked like shit and felt sloppy and unkempt the whole time.

Why are you doing this? asked my husband-to-be.
Because I want to wear hair extensions—I have a plan.
Can't you wear a wig?
Absolutely not—that wouldn't look real.
And this will?

What did he know? I ignored him and went to have a look at how much my hair had grown in the past few hours. Staring at myself in the mirror I realized I didn't even look like myself. But that was good, wasn't it? I was getting married and this was an integral part of the costume, the drama queen in me committed to it completely. I was Russell Crowe in *The Insider*, De Niro in *Raging Bull* and Renée Zellwegger in *Bridget Jones's Diary*—anything for the character.

The horror that was my hair helped me scale back the amount of mental space I was able to dedicate to the outfit search and this turned out to be a blessing in disguise. I started making quick decisions. First up, I decided I was going to wear red. It should have been the obvious choice considering it is the colour that almost every Indian bride wears. I had been avoiding it precisely for this reason but now I didn't have the time to be unique, I had my back up against a wall and at least red didn't bring out the yellow in my skin tone. I also decided that I would have to wear a sari because with my body type a salwaar-kameez or lehenga would make me look like a drag queen.

Then the woman who was actually doing all the dirty work called me.

I have found a beautiful temple sari, it's red and gold, very traditional. Very. My mum was fed up, she had suffered through several sari purchases, all of which I had turned my nose up at and by this time I was done too. I was like the British by the time Mahatma Gandhi came along—there was no fight left in me. Plus I *wanted* tradition, didn't I? And what could be more appropriate than a sari made in a temple.

It's not really made in a temple, my mother informed me, *but it's very traditional, and Ruchika and Anandi have seen it and love it.*

My mother is a clever woman, telling me my friends liked it was obviously a smart move.

My research on temple saris showed me that this was what most Tamilian brides worth their salt wore. Perfect, because on the tradition scale these women were very high up in my estimation—I would be a Tamilian bride. The only thing decidedly non-Tamil would be my blouse. Like a mullet it would be business in the front, party in the back. Backless sari blouses were my thing and I wanted to maintain some semblance of who I really was—a woman who believed that her upper back was her best feature. To round it all off I had arranged to borrow Anuli's wedding jewellery, because it was beautiful, traditional. And free.

The week before the wedding I was introduced to the groom's

family. My mother-in-law, who had only ever seen me in my regular clothes, was a little concerned about what I would be wearing. I explained my south Indian-themed costume and assured her that the sari in question was 'very heavy', words Ruchika in her wisdom had instructed me to use, which seemed to put her mind immediately at ease. I then proceeded to inform her that south Indian brides did not cover their heads and hence I would be following suit. I won't lie, I thought my decision was rather feminist and brave, especially given that telling this to a Jat mother-in-law was like telling Jesus that you didn't believe in God. Now that I think about it I may have had my feminist awakening right around the time my mostly unfeminist dreams were coming together.

HERE COMES THE BRIDE

Our wedding day finally arrived. I woke up in a terrible mood. I was the only person under sixty in the entire wedding party who had gone to bed early. All my friends had stayed out until sunrise at a party thrown by a friend of ours, which I had avoided only because I knew that without a full eight hours of sleep, I would look my age—a role I wasn't playing that day. My bad mood was made worse because Thaks had also attended the party and was one of the last to leave. I hoped he looked like shit.

After fighting with him on the phone and eating some breakfast, I headed with my mother to Madonna, a salon where I was to have my false hair attached. Waiting for me at Madonna was Rajkumar, a middle-aged, rotund, effeminate south Indian man. I was a little afraid of having a man do my hair but his obvious homosexuality made me feel a lot better—not to stereotype or anything but if someone knew drama it would be a gay hairstylist. I stopped feeling better and started feeling worse when his assistant Dorai paraded in, swinging his tight little ass from side to side, and offering me a basket of rather dead-looking jasmine flowers and a truckload of really dead-looking false hair. After I made a fuss about the flowers, Dorai was dispatched to find more alive looking ones while Rajkumar surveyed me and my stringy hair. I could tell he wasn't pleased with what he had to work with.

How you want it?

I want a bun, I said authoritatively, *keep it low, on the nape of my neck and then attach the flowers in a circle.* I was hoping that my explanation would suffice, and was kicking myself for not having carried the picture of Feroze Gujral in a jewellery advertisement that I was modelling my hairstyle on. Feroze, of course, is my generation's answer to Cindy Crawford—a supermodel type who can carry any hairstyle. I have no idea what I was thinking.

Rajkumar examined me some more and got to work. He used what must have been 400 pins to secure what was surely 400 pounds of hair to my head. He weaved, braided, and gelled every lock of it into submission. I could not see what was going on behind me but I could feel my head getting heavier. An hour later he was done when in waltzed Dorai with his less dead flowers that were promptly attached to my head. Together, they stood back, presented me with a hand mirror, and with a flourish swivelled me around to admire my new look.

It was a disaster. Attached to the back of my skull was not a graceful little bun as I had envisioned but a gigantic French loaf wreathed in a garland of mildly wilting jasmines.

It's v-very big, I stammered.

Actually, it looks very nice, very traditional. This was my mother, offering the one word she hoped would calm me down. Besides, she was responsible for getting me back to the hotel and knew that undoing Rajkumar's creation was not an option.

With Rajkumar, Dorai and my mother silently pressuring me to let it go I reluctantly gave up the fight, and balancing my head that now weighed several extra pounds, stalked out of Madonna. Never to return.

Waiting for us in our room were Anandi and Ruch, my friends who were in charge of my make-up and overall state of mind, and my dad.

Doesn't her hair look great? trilled my mother in an effort to pre-empt any sort of cock-up in the form of an honest opinion.

While my dad sat there trying to rearrange his facial features to read neutral rather than horror, my girlfriends, the professional liars that they are, went on and on about how fantastic I looked, and that, yes, it was a little big but so what, and no it was not utterly ridiculous.

At this point I excused myself and went to the bathroom to have a good look at the thing. On the upside it was so heavy that it had pulled my face back thus acting like a facelift, on the downside, however, it wasn't big, it was enormous—the damn thing was practically the size of my own head. I was devastated. Sure, I had lived through a plethora of crappy hairstyles, including one that my friend Kusum had called the 'Anil Kapoor', but did I really have to endure one today! I couldn't even shake my head in disgust because I might have broken my neck. I took a deep breath, told myself the show must go on, and went back outside hoping that Anandi would transform me and my two heads into a vision of beauty and glamour.

It is a fact that good foundation and red lipstick will brighten the worst day, and my sari was quite exquisite. The overall effect made me forget about the calamity on my scalp so when I heard Thaks talking loudly to some friends in the corridor I foolishly decided to get his opinion on how lovely I looked. I rushed out to find him standing there dressed in his wedding finery, turban, sword and all.

What do you think?

With the look of someone searching for the least awful thing to say he responded, *You look like a Bharatanatyam dancer.*

I fled back to my room and yelled at my mother, father and friends. I dared not cry because Anandi had done a rather artistic job of my eyes. Once I was done ranting and raving, I calmed down and thought—screw it, at least it's traditional, now all I have to do is make sure the photographer doesn't get any pictures of me in profile.

I needn't have worried my now over-sized head about that.

When the ceremony began I made my way to the mandap. As I seated myself in front of the ancient pujari, who looked in dire need of a nap, or a drink, or both, my mother-in-law swooped down and threw a spectacular, bejeweled chunni over my head. As far as she was concerned I could take my feminist ideas and shove them where the sun didn't shine. Or maybe, just maybe, she was trying to cover up Rajkumar's ruin.

SEXY TIME

As we all know, in our motherland wedding ceremonies are followed by yet another ceremony called the 'suhaag raat'. This is the first night the couple spends together and the night they 'officially' consummate their relationship. Per Indian tradition, the expectation is that both bride and groom are still virgins, or at the very least the bride. The suhaag raat is the night on which the virginal wife submits herself to her husband for a deflowering of epic proportions. It is a night of rose petals, almond milk, lovingly stained bedsheets, fake orgasms and, in many cases, fake virginity as well. Because my man and I had celebrated our respective 'first times' a very long time ago things were a little different for us.

After the ceremony there was the reception, the sole purpose of which was to make sure everyone got access to alcohol. While most of us focused our efforts on getting loaded, two of my more juvenile friends, Dhruva and Benjy, decided to honour the less formal, but equally idiotic, tradition of laying waste to, aka 'decorating', the bridal suite. These top-shelf morons had stolen four massive planters and a housekeeping trolley and installed them in our room. Their genius move was viewed by the hotel security on the security cameras and so as soon as they were done depositing all this in our room, the staff promptly came and took it back.

At about two in the morning the DJ timed out and a bunch of us went back to our room to try and stretch the evening out. About an hour later everyone left and Thaks, who had outdone himself, took off all his clothes and instantly passed out. I could not do that and instead had to waste another age taking off my hair. This involved the removal of all 400 pins that Rajkumar, the bastard, had used to keep his creation in place. Eventually I fell into bed, drunk and in need of a good sound sleep.

At some point shortly after this our phone rang. Now everyone knows that in the fragile condition brought about by copious amounts of alcohol and no sleep a ringing phone can sound like an air raid siren, and induce the same level of panic. On top of this, I was completely disoriented by my surroundings. *Yes*, I gasped, as I pounced on the phone, hoping that I could at least save one of us from waking. I need not have worried about that, Thaks was dead to the world.

Good morning, madam, came the painfully chipper response, *this is the 6 a.m. wake-up call you had asked for. We hope you had a comfortable night.*

Clearly Dhruva and Benjy, disappointed that their previous lame prank had been dismantled, had set this nonsense up. I was in more pain than I care to remember. I wanted to kill someone, but I managed to thank the receptionist and fell back to sleep. Then, at 7 a.m. the doorbell rang. Cursing and swearing I yelled at Thaks to get his butt out of bed and see what was going on. I had no intention of moving and lay there, my face in my pillow, fighting what felt like an intense bout of seasickness.

Slowly, and very reluctantly, Thaks, who, as far as I was concerned, should have leapt out of bed now that he was my husband, got up, and absentmindedly pulled on a waist-length t-shirt. He then stumbled to the door and together with his full monty on display greeted the room service waiter who had brought us the breakfast we had supposedly ordered.

We didn't order this.
Sir, it was ordered from your room last night.
Rads—what do I do?

I don't know, I wailed from under the covers.

We don't want it. Sorry about all this, our friends were being stupid. He apologized profusely with his bangers and mash still staring the waiter in his face.

Okay, sir.

Thaks closed the door and came back into the room. Suddenly, a thought occurred to my frugal lord and he rushed back, opened the door, stepped out in to the corridor and yelled after the waiter.

Excuse me!

Yes, sir? the man nervously turned around, probably hoping Thaks had his pants on—but, of course, he did not.

And then my husband asked the most relevant question, and one that speaks volumes for the man he is.

Has the food been paid for?

Because even hung-over, sleep deprived and half-naked, there was no way he was going to let good money and food go to waste. Lucky me. I had so much to look forward to.

THE BABY QUESTION

Are you really a woman if you have not had a child?
This question was put to me by my cousin when I informed him I wasn't planning to have one. Yes, my cousin is a Neanderthal but he is not alone in his primitive thinking. He was simply verbalizing what most people around me were thinking.

As a woman in India the decision to have children, like marriage, is no decision at all, it's a given. We live in a society that tells us that being a mother is inextricably linked to being a woman and that if you happen to be female and in possession of an able body and a relatively sound mind then the general consensus is that you should create life. And, it's not like people stop at thinking we *should* have kids. No! They think we should *want* to have them. Regardless of our circumstances all of us must feel the mythical maternal urge and immediately convert that urge into a baby. I wanted this urge, I wanted it bad, and I had been assured I would have it. I even thought I had it once, just before my period. But I quickly realized that I was just horny—a feeling profound enough to convince anyone that she wants babies.

Then some mothers came out and said that they had never felt the maternal instinct at all, that it was a lot of hot air. Others admitted to not being able to bond with their baby for months on end. Still others copped to horrendous post-partum depression, some confessing to wanting to kill their baby, and very sadly some of them did. Yet despite what seemed to me like mounting evidence that not every single one of us should procreate, I was being told to go for it. After all how else was I to prove I was a woman.

Motherhood has always been a big deal. Back in the day it was sanctified, today it is straight-up glamorized. Even Angelina Jolie, stealer of Jennifer Aniston's husband, endorsed this point of view. Ages ago, in an interview that I read in my beloved *People* magazine, Angie said that she became a woman only after she adopted Maddox of Cambodia. I have no idea what the fuck she was before that, by the way, because if she wasn't a woman then we might as well all pack it in right now. I always thought she was a woman. In fact, I thought she was *the* woman. I used to imagine that if I pulled Angelina's knickers off I would find myself gazing upon the world's most womanly vagina. A Perfect 10 pussy. A pussy with an archway covered in exotic flowers, a pussy with light French music playing delicately in the background, and where little pussy people played happily all day.

As for me and my less than perfect punani—I never wanted kids. Ever. But I never had the courage to say so. As an inherent people pleaser I just could not bring myself to hurt other people's feelings. And to be completely honest, telling people I didn't want kids felt like I was doing just that.

But why? they would ask with a look that was a mixture of disappointment and pain, like I was depriving not just myself but them too of something very valuable.

I don't know why, I would reply miserably, because while I knew I was telling them the truth I also knew this would not be a suitable response.

What do you mean you 'don't know'? This is a big decision, you have to know why.

Do we really need to know why? Isn't it enough that we believe it for ourselves? Nope! See, ladies, we live in a world that is accustomed to the likes of Angelina Jolie—women who can't STFU about how awesomesauce parenting is—and so when they come up against a chick who doesn't want any part of that, they can't understand it. They need to know why, they need a reason and I didn't have one because I was going on instinct and my instinct was telling me that I wasn't really interested in being a mum.

But try telling someone that and watch as they recoil in horror. Then, they recover themselves, not because they realize they are being rude but because they know that they have been sent to you by the universe to convince you to change your mind. And, finally, they invest a shocking number of hours over the rest of their lifetime in telling you why you are wrong.

Rads, at the end of the day it is your decision; we just want to make sure you don't regret it.

Ah regret! I have no idea why people fear it so much. I have so many things I regret—I regret I ever smoked my first cigarette, I regret I like sugar, I regret that I never learnt how to speak Hindi properly. My inventory of regrets alone could fill this chapter and the next; yet here I am leading a relatively happy life. Adding a baby, or a lack thereof, to this burgeoning list didn't bother me one bit. But it bothered everyone else because as far as they were concerned they weren't poking their long noses into my private business, they were performing an intervention, to save me from myself and my godawful choice to remain childless.

So instead of telling people to go fuck themselves, like I should have, I started rooting around for a reason that they would like. I knew I would have to think logically because clearly my feelings on the matter were inconsequential. The first reason I came up with was my husband.

Why can't we just say you don't want a baby? I implored.

Why me? he countered.

Because it's not weird when a guy says he doesn't want kids, it's expected. In fact, we find it weird when some of you do want babies.

That's sexist, by the way.

Yes, but can we just say it's you?
No, we can't because it's not true.
So you want a baby?
I'm just saying it could be nice.

Oh, bugger off, I thought. I am not having a baby because it 'could be nice'. What was his problem? Why couldn't he just back me up on this one? It took me a while but over time I realized why he couldn't. Having a baby or not having one was not his decision. It was mine. There isn't a single couple where when it comes to having a baby the man's decision counted in any real way. Couples who have babies usually have them because the woman involved is determined to do so. The only time a man's POV counts is if he is a domineering, insecure jackass with no respect for you or your body. Most men think it would be 'nice' and then go along with whatever you want. Unfortunately, this thought came to me very recently so at the time of his refusal I did not have a particularly generous view of him. Instead, I thought him to be a selfish person with no sympathy for the turmoil I was in. And so not being able to count on Thaks I was moved to seek an alternative excuse.

Children are too expensive, we can't afford it, I gleefully announced.

Oh please! Your mother and I raised you on practically nothing.

I know, Pops, I was there, and I hated it. Why do people think it's a noble sacrifice to bring up children in a frugal manner? It's never fun for the child and I am going to guess it is even less so for the parents. Anyway, it was clear that monetary reasoning wasn't getting me anywhere so I went with the pain and aggravation defence.

I am afraid of childbirth. My vagina is a one-way street. I am okay with things going in, I just don't want anything coming back out.

Oh please! Women have been doing it for centuries. You'll be fine.

This is not true at all. I have cross-questioned friends who have had natural deliveries, drug-assisted ones and C-sections. All of them have felt excruciating pain that in some cases lasted for days. But the agony of childbirth is what people think of as a medal and so my not wanting the medal just made me feel like some under-achiever.

At my age wouldn't it be dangerous? I was at this stage closer to forty.

Rads! I have a cousin in London and she had a kid at forty-seven. Forty-seven! Isn't that amazing!

What I continue to find truly amazing is the fact that there is always some crusty old crone somewhere or the other, squeezing one out at the last minute thus making the rest of us look like inadequate sissies. Everyone it seems has a friend who, against all odds, created life while she had one high-heeled hoof in the grave and the other on a banana peel.

But I really knew I was over the hill when people stopped asking me for my reasons and instead started to give me reasons to have a baby. One kind friend took the trouble to drop me a note via Facebook.

Radhika, you really should have kids. It will take your relationship to the next level.

What 'next level' I wanted to scream! The level of sleepless nights and zero disposable income? Is being constantly tired and borderline broke supposed to make us more in love or something? And what makes you think that as a couple we haven't already reached that level of pain and anxiety? Perhaps we did it without having kids! Maybe that is how fabulous we are. Did anyone think of that?

But it wasn't her fault. She, like the rest of us, is hardwired to encourage childbirth. We have been made to believe that a baby is basically a magical agent of change and that having one will, in one fell swoop, make your husband love you more, make your life more meaningful and, above all else, is the best thing you will ever do as a woman. I didn't care about any of it. I was perfectly content to continue with my low-level relationship and just as happy with my seemingly meaningless existence. I will admit to being offended by most people's assumption that the best we ladies could do was have children. Really? So I guess we should just scrub Madame Curie, Mary Kom and Malala Yousafzai—and that's just the biyatches in my 'M' directory of kick-ass females.

The more I think about it, the more I am convinced that human beings are just scared of any deviation from what is tried-and-tested, they are afraid that the world will come to an abrupt end unless everyone follows the same path. In general, we are unable to, never mind respect, but even ignore anyone whose life choices are different from our own. Including my mum-in-law who happens to be a mummy four times over.

Beta, bachche paida karlo. Deepak bhi settle down ho jayega.

Apparently my man-sized adult husband was in an unsettled state that had somehow become my problem. And I almost took this seriously until it dawned upon me that it wasn't just NOT my problem, it was her fault! Look all you MILs out there—take a seat. If your pride and joy isn't settled down, then guess what—that's on you. You messed it up, and my having a baby with a grown-up who is still unsettled (your words, sister, not mine) is not very feminist advice now is it?

But all this browbeating absolutely pales in comparison to the final, and quite frankly most persuasive argument for procreation: *You will die alone!* A fear-based tactic and the only one that really freaked me out. All I could see was me in an assisted living facility where I am the only resident with no visitors. I described this distressing scenario to my husband who assured me that I had nothing to worry about because I was most certainly going to die before him due to my weakling constitution (both mental and physical) and hence I would be an encumbrance but most certainly not alone.

Anyhow, the point is that when you want to do something that isn't the 'norm' you will be made to feel like you have a problem and if you hear it often enough then you start to believe it too. At some point I started to question my own choice. I figured that if everyone wanted to know why I didn't want kids and if all my reasons were being brushed off with the same determination used to get rid of dog hair on black velvet jeans, then something had to be wrong with me. And so I did what any woman who is afraid she is not a woman does—I made an appointment with my gynaecologist. Now here is the thing, I have never been pregnant. Not once in my entire life, not even in college when my preferred mode of contraception was three magic words: please pull out.

What I was hoping would happen is that I would go over there, she would rummage about in my folds and then she would inform me that I was physically incapable of baby production. I am aware that this is usually terrible news for women and I do not make light of it, but it is, in my experience, the only thing that will shut people up. Even the worst busybodies are silenced by the level of awkwardness generated by the words 'I can't have kids'—so much better than 'I don't want kids'.

I couldn't wait; now instead of debate I would generate sympathy. It's true, look around you, have you seen the way people react to a woman who tells them she can't have children? They feel sorry for us! Because to them we have the most chronic of all disabilities, not being able to birth life reduces us to a state of helpless misery, we are now these sad, useless little creatures with no arms or legs, just an empty stump of a body that your martyr husband can push around in a little wheelchair. Ah, and what a nice man he is to remain with you despite your obvious dysfunction.

And so it was in a rather optimistic state of mind that I set off to see Dr Susan Lehr, MD—my Lady-Bits Physician, a lovely person, with an equally lovely office that overlooked Central Park. We exchanged the usual pleasantries and then got right into it.

Is your period regular?

Oh yes. Very! I answered proudly.

And when was your last period?

I, err, don't exactly recall. I could sense her disapproval and she was correct to feel it. Sexually active women should have the dates of their menstrual cycle at their fingertips. I went from pride to shame in seconds.

And how long have you been trying to have a baby?

Ever since everyone started badgering me about it, I wanted to say but I had a feeling this was not what she was looking for.

About six months, I lied.

And what steps have you taken in that direction?

WTF. This was beginning to feel like my twelfth grade final exams—I was utterly unprepared for it. The only steps we had taken was to have unprotected sex but by now I knew Dr Susan wanted a more sophisticated response. Luckily my blank expression pushed her to be more specific.

When do you have sex? she asked.

Ah! This I could handle.

Usually on Sunday, I replied, and then just to be amusing I added, *I try and get it out of the way by noon.*

Dr Susan smiled politely, *No, I meant have you been having sex on your oestrogen surge dates?*

Obviously bloody not, Dr Susan, because as you can probably tell by the look on my face today is the first time I have ever even heard of such a thing. But I did not say that, instead I sat there silently, my cheeks ablaze with embarrassment. None of this was as straightforward as I thought it would be, Dr Susan hadn't even asked me to take my pants off yet—wasn't she supposed to check my plumbing? And why was her tone of voice starting to resemble one usually employed when communicating with a sweet but slow-witted person?

So the next time you have your period make sure to write those dates down in your day planner, okay?

I resolved to purchase a planner as soon as I left her office.

Okay good! Now once you do that then chart your oestrogen surge dates—it's very simple.

I would Google 'oestrogen surge dates' as soon as possible.

Then all you have to do is have sex on your surge dates. I would say try that for about twelve months and then if you have no result come back and we will figure something out.

What the fuck? This whole charting of dates thing sounded slightly more tedious than a Scandinavian visa application. Of course Dr Susan was doing me a favour, the tests that would actually yield any information about the state of my reproductive system were invasive and probably painful. Her packing me off to do the necessary groundwork was probably the responsible thing to do. I left in a state of high stress. This visit was supposed to have solved all my problems; now I had what sounded like a year's worth of homework and still no reason. What the hell was I to tell people?

They say that when one door closes another one opens. Dr Susan may not have given me my reason but now I had information that I could wield to my advantage, and by that I mean I could convincingly lie that I was in fact TRYING to get pregnant.

That was the first question Dr Susan had asked me and that is what I would say was happening. Plus now I had lingo like 'oestrogen surge dates' in my arsenal, who was going to challenge that?

Hi, Rad, how are you and Thaks doing?

Oh wonderful, thanks, and then lowering my voice as if in confidence, *we are trying, by the way.*

It is truly fascinating that when a middle-aged woman says that she is 'trying' she need not elaborate on what. People instantly know that she is not trying to repot her plants, or trying to lose weight, or trying to learn origami but that she is trying to fulfil her highest potential as a woman, and their excited reactions never failed to disappoint.

And so that became my standard reply to any and all questions thrown at me about my plans for parenthood and it worked like a charm—now, instead of getting the third degree, people were practically celebrating me! This was certainly something I could get used to. Unfortunately, I could not do any such thing because pretending that you are trying gives you respite for a year tops. After which, if you have nothing to show for it, then people start making some assumptions about you.

And the first assumption that they are going to make is that you are not trying hard enough.

Rads, you know what, it's not easy for everyone to get pregnant. But for me and Rohit it was very easy, she was quick to clarify, *all three on the first try itself, can you imagine?!*

I am still unable to understand the heavy-duty pride 'high fertility' couples feel. It's comical!

But for my poor sister-in-law—for their second one they tried for more than two years.

Ah, the sweet smell of success made sweeter still by another's failure.

First, she went through intra-cytoplasmic sperm injections, did not work. Then, gamete intrafallopian transfer, that also did not work, and then, finally, zygote intrafallopian transfers, thank god that worked. It's very painful but so worth it. They have twins now. Can you pass that channa dal, please.

The sub-text of this dinner party conversation was loud and clear—try harder, you twat.

The other assumption people will make, and one that I find rather entertaining, is that your husband must be gay. Or 'a gay' as we like to say in India. *He is a gay. That is why there is no issue.* This is one of the stupidest things I have ever heard because the fact is that gay men have been marrying and having babies with straight women for centuries—mechanically, it is entirely possible. That said, like many husbands of childless women my husband is not a gay. Sure he can sometimes behave like a bit of a gaandu, but he is definitely not a gay.

And, finally, an assumption that was repeatedly made about me—if you don't have children then you are a child hater. This I was offended by. How dare anyone think that? What did they know about me to assume this? With my self-righteous undies knotted up I went out of my way to dispel this idea. I would refrain from complaining about noisy kids on an aircraft, I would spout rubbish like, 'there are no bad kids, just bad parents'. I even found myself encouraging mothers to talk about their kids at parties much to the horror of my friend Ani who despite having two children of her own is loathe to discuss kidstuff.

Rads, I don't want to hear another word about that idiot woman's son.

Oh, she's harmless, I tittered.

I don't give a shit—I didn't come out to talk about kids. I spent the whole damn day with mine.

All very well for Ani to mouth off like this, I thought, she had kids. I, on the other hand, did not and felt I needed to prove to people I wasn't a bad person. Women who hate kids are lumped in the same group as fur-wearers and wife-beaters. I didn't need that kind of PR.

But I had to accept that I was over-compensating. Truthfully, I hated being seated next to a baby on a flight, some kids are assholes regardless of how nice their parents are, and the only time I encourage a parent to talk about children is when he or she has displayed an overwhelming lack of conversational skills. It wasn't that I hated children exactly but I will admit that I find small kids highly overrated. They are just not as cute or clever as the world makes them out to be and I find their hobbies and interests only slightly less mind numbing than watching paint dry. And at least paint has those fumes. All of this dawned upon me the afternoon that I was forced to spend several hours in the company of Anuli's six-year-old daughter and her BFF. At first, things were going well. The kids were in their room and I was out in the living area minding my own business. My meditative state was rudely destroyed when the two cretins came galloping out of their space and into mine.

Aunty Radhika, they squeaked, breathless with excitement, *will you come watch our dance.*

My first reaction was to tell them to piss off but I didn't want the 'child hater' persona to follow me so I did what people who love children do. I allowed them to lead me to their lair.

Aunty Radhika, you stand here. Why do children's rooms have nothing but that idiotic miniature furniture?

And we will do the dance over here. 'Over here' was behind a bed so now I was supposed to give them my feedback on choreography I was only able to watch from the knees up.

Aunty Radhika, we don't have any music. This was already going badly. *But we will show you our steps. Are you ready?*

And then they started dancing. This performance would have been tedious enough to get through with music, without musical accompaniment it was unbearable. One kid sort of knew the steps because she had made them up, the other one's head was swivelling about like the actress in *Poltergeist* because she didn't know the steps and so no matter what direction she was facing she had to keep her eyes on the leader. As I watched them, hoping that neither planned to give up her day job, I suddenly noticed both of them looking at me expectantly. What they were seeking was encouragement and it is what lovers of children everywhere are supposed to give kids no matter the quality of the show before them.

And so, despite my worst intentions, I started to clap and smile in a supportive manner, and as I stood there watching these two small, talentless, mouth-breathers, I began to think about something. See, I could walk out of that room and never have to see those two ever again if I so chose, but the mothers were stuck there forever watching that godawful dance in a never-ending, nightmarish loop. And given the amount of time, effort and dance lessons that it takes to raise a child who in all likelihood would end up like one of these two twerps, how come when a woman says she wants a baby no one ever asks 'why?'

MOTHER PRESSURE IS
THE NEW PEER PRESSURE

Oh Vazi, you should have at least one, you would make such a great mom!

I am convinced that the only people as pushy as a parent trying to switch you over to their side are cocaine users. And how about if I were just an average mom? Would that do? Probably not. And right here we have a reason some people may not want to join the parenting ranks—too much pressure.

Thanks to Catherine Zeta-Jones I will always think of success as nothing less than being pregnant while winning an Oscar. She epitomizes what the media has been telling women in recent years: that we can have it all. Yards of copy and hours of debate have been dedicated to this idea and the upshot is that if we ladies are clever and very hardworking then we can have both a baby and a career. It's not like the olden times when a woman had to choose—today we are being told she can have both. Of course, I have asked some of my friends who do have jobs and children if they have it all. *I don't know about anyone else,* wailed a mother of two, *all I know is there are some nights I come home and all I want to do is eat my bloody kids.*

The truth is I don't have the work ethic it takes to be a great mother. I may, on the other hand, have what it takes to be a dad.

Think about it, a dad has it all. For one thing he does not have to get pregnant, he doesn't have to sacrifice the joys of drugs and alcohol for the requisite amount of time it takes to bake a baby. He can go out and get shit-faced and not worry that some little girl is going to have a hand sticking out of her head because of alcohol poisoning. If men had to quit smoking, drinking and drugging for even just the nine months it takes to grow a kid—never mind the whole run-up to getting pregnant and then the breast-feeding time afterwards—just the nine months—we would be extinct.

Then, there is maternal guilt that no father is ever going to have to deal with. As a dad no one will ever judge you unless you mess things up big time, and by that I mean you need to really go out of your way to be a prick. There needs to be alcoholism, wife-beating, cheating, or jail for someone to call you a bad dad. And even then I have actually heard people say, 'I grant you he was a shitty husband but he is a wonderful father'. For the mothers, on the other hand, not giving your kid her cough medicine on time makes you unworthy.

Do you think working dads sit around at work worrying about how they can get back home in time to play with the kids, help with their homework, feed them, bathe them and put them to bed so that the child feels loved and won't turn into a junkie, pole dancing, anorexic? No—of course not! And you know why? Because the moms already have that covered. These women are damned if they do and damned if they don't. They have advice coming at them from everywhere, their friends, mothers, sisters, mothers-in-law, blogs, websites, magazines and books. Everyone thinks they know how it's done and they keep heaping more pain and aggravation on the moms of the world.

A friend Facebooked an article about a working mum who had hired someone to read to her children so that she could get some free time, or 'me time' as she described it to the interviewer. The post received two reactions. The majority believed that this was a cop-out and that she was 'buying' her way out of motherhood. There was genuine anger over the fact that this educated, smart woman would leave the important task of reading to her kids to someone else—regardless of how qualified the reader was, in this particular case a young PhD in child psychology (talk about being over-qualified for the job). Reading, it seems, is a bonding experience for mother and child and only an ogre would relinquish this task to another. It goes without saying that all of the women who commented were mothers themselves.

Then there was the minority reaction, and one that describes my own personal view: are you bitches kidding me?

Let's be honest already! Women have been outsourcing childcare since the dawn of time, and if you can allow another person to bathe, feed, dress and drive your brat to school, surely someone else reading to them can't be that far behind. As far as I am concerned, once you have accepted that a nanny can wash your child's bum, you are all in. Like it or not, you have crossed a line that no longer affords you the right to decide how another woman decides to raise her child. Are you people that keyed up that you can't stand to see a guilt-free, hands-off colleague enjoying a moment of peace and quiet? Motherhood has moved from being a calling to being a job to being what it is today—a competition, and the winner is that magical female who works full-time and then presumably rushes home to read to her kids despite the fact that she is exhausted.

And, finally, my favourite part of being a dad—you can become fat and bald and no one will ever say *Wow, he really let himself go after the baby*. Look around you. Where are the hot dads? Thanks to my close association with many mothers, I have been forced into several children's birthday parties and there are always a bunch of hot moms, being all hot and sexy for the kids and the other moms. You know the type—the ones who smugly managed to knock off all the baby weight and wear tight T-shirts, tucked INTO their jeans, *Oh my god, after Suhaila, the weight just came off, no problem at all. I am very lucky like that! See!*

Loads of hot mommies, but no hot dads. Instead we have a

bunch of middle-aged guys in those awful dad-sandals and flappy shorts, swilling beer and not even trying to hold in their guts.

If I am ever a parent I am going to have to be a dad.

EPILOGUE

You get out what you put in. Except with Isabgol.

I never thought I would be a comedian, I thought I would be a corporate raider. I didn't know what that meant but I had seen Michael Douglas in *Wall Street* and Richard Gere in *Pretty Woman* and I knew that it involved money, power and hookers. I wanted this to be my life. And if things had worked out that way I would not be writing this epilogue. Instead, I would be snorting cocaine off Julia Roberts' bottom. This, by the way, is a scene they decided to cut from the film so they could get an R rating—because every mother should be able to show her daughter that being a prostitute will one day pay off big time. Incidentally, prostitution was my Plan B but when push came to shove I was too middle-class for it.

Eventually I made the discovery, or maybe it was an admission, that I was a performer. This happened in my thirties. Look, some of us are late bloomers, what can I tell you?

That said, comedy specifically was not a conscious decision. I slipped into it. And the starting point of this slip that became a slide that has since become a free-fall started in 2001 when I moved to New York City. As you should know by now, I lived with my boyfriend and every day I would go to work, hit the gym, and then come home expecting to be entertained. I was in a new, rather overwhelming city. I had few friends, no money and my first year there was lived with the daily dread of deportation. It was right after 9/11, people were being fired left and right, and I was in a funk. I was depressed and I was being depressing.

Which is why my boyfriend-who-is-now-my-husband sat me down one evening and explained that he had a goal. He was going to run the New York City Marathon in a few months and he would be training intensively for it. Then he asked me what I planned to do with my spare time. *Isn't there anything you want to do? Any classes you want to take? This is New York, you can do anything.*

He was right.

I have always wanted to learn French or something.

Or something. This was utter rubbish, I had the opportunity to learn both French and Hindi in school and I had frittered it away. The result, as my father loves to put it, is that I now speak two languages—Poor Quality Hindi and Poor Quality English. Anyhow, there wasn't a chance in hell I was actually going to sit down and try that on again. But I had to say something—who did he think he was with his stupid goals?

We left it at that but the seed of embarrassment had been planted. I wondered what classes to take. Languages had obviously been eliminated. I briefly considered a gourmet cooking class, and I even thought about running the fucking marathon. But I knew that all of this was either too much work, too much work or too much work. Then something happened that changed my life.

Halle Berry won an Academy Award for *Monster's Ball* and watching this brown girl with short hair weep through her acceptance speech made me think I too could be a highly successful dramatic actress. In order to become an Academy Award winner I decided to take up acting lessons. It sounded glamorous and far less taxing than conjugating verbs. I had no idea at the time how hard it would be to become any kind of actor, least of all an award-winning one. In hindsight, I realize I should have probably stuck to languages, but that is the beauty of life, if we ever knew in advance how hard something was likely to be we wouldn't do it.

And so off I went to an acting school in New York's West Village. HB Studio is a well-known institution amongst the city's acting community—it's cheap, you can take just one class at a time, and literally anyone can join. This last one being the cornerstone of every institution, academic or otherwise, that I have been part of.

My first time there was on a Thursday night after work. It was pouring rain that evening and I almost didn't go. But the idea of being the chick with no life of her own was really bothering me so I hitched up my big girl bloomers, bought a three-dollar umbrella from the entrepreneur outside the subway stop and shoved off. It was a cold night and I remember this well because I was inappropriately dressed. I was in standard ad executive gear—black trousers and black turtleneck but instead of a jacket I had thrown on, of all things, a black and red Kashmiri firan. It was a ridiculous choice from a practical and visual standpoint and my colleagues had made fun of me all day at work (one told me I looked like a dykey priest). But as soon as I stepped into the HB Studio administration office I knew I was home because a bottle-blonde, hippy-looking woman told me how fantastic I looked and how great my 'tunic' was. I thanked her and then found my way to the admissions desk.

My objective was to grab the school prospectus and then go home and fantasize about winning an Oscar for a few weeks. After that I would decide on what classes I wanted to take. It was a slow night and there was just one other person there for the same thing. I wish I remembered her name rather than what I was wearing but I don't. I do recall that she was Latina, older than me and a mother of three. Her kids were grown and she needed something to do. I suspected her husband may have shamed her into it but then I realized that not all women need to be pushed to accomplish things—some do so with no prodding whatsoever and she was one of them. I learnt this the hard way.

As we were both climbing down the beautiful wooden

stairwell, complaining bitterly about the weather we were about to expose ourselves to, we noticed a massive poster advertising a free improv class with a teacher from Los Angeles. The class was due to start in less than ten minutes and despite the instructor's impeccable resume I most certainly wasn't going to impulsively attend it. I had to go home as planned and sit on my arse. But women who accomplish things on their own do not take kindly to this type of reasoning and the next thing I knew my Latina pal and I were standing in Holly Mandel's improv class, at the end of which she left and I signed up for the season. It was a no-brainer. There were no lines to learn—I could not possibly ask for less.

I didn't know this then but Holly would one day be not only my coach but also a creative collaborator and the person who convinced me to teach improv—a skill I treasure, not just because I can earn a living from it but because it allows me to spread the idea that the unknown is fun and that taking a risk, even if you fall flat on your face, is better than sitting still. Thanks to improv, I learned to write sketch comedy, then I wrote comedy monologues, and then I strung those monologues together into my first one-woman show. I didn't know any of this would happen. Like I said, I was on track to win an Oscar, something I still fully intend to do the moment I am cast in a biopic about Indira Gandhi where I will play Jawaharlal Nehru.

Improv taught me a few other things as well. It taught me to focus on what is happening right now and to let go of the stuff I can't control. Like aging. Age and its consequences can play havoc with a woman's mind. It can make you hate anyone under twenty-five and, far worse, it can make you hate yourself. It is harder on pretty people so at least I didn't have that problem but it's still tough. Your face and ass both start to loosen up at the exact same time and people notice this and call you ma'am and Aunty. But you can actually escape this burning building if you find something, anything, which has nothing to do with how you look or how old you are. And for me this life raft is comedy.

Comedy gave me a career, it gave me a sense of accomplishment, and it gave me confidence. In the words of a Victoria's Secret supermodel (I don't know which one, I was too busy staring at her thigh gap) 'there is nothing more sexy than confidence'. I believe this. It's not about being an egomaniac, or about being the best. It's about learning to love what you can do without worrying too much about what everyone else is up to. I still have bad days. Like that day when I had to share the gym with Shahid Kapoor. Have you seen how YOUNG and PRETTY he is? Then I remembered I am funny. And I went back to my squats.

ACKNOWLEDGEMENTS

Marina Romashko my idea coach, you were the first person who told me to write a book. 'It does not have to be great' was the encouraging way in which you put it. This not-great book is pretty much your fault.

Simar Puneet, my editor, for guiding me away from a nervous breakdown on more than one occasion. You are sweet, clever and have the same bad habits I do.

To the team at Aleph Book Company for helping me push this baby out into the world.

My girlfriends in India and across the world without whom I would have nothing—no clothes, make-up or jewellery—and above all, no stories. You girls are my life and even if I did have a real sister I would love you more.

Gayatri Singh and Swanzal Kak for providing office space and sisterlove when I first arrived in Gurgaon. Without you this book and my marriage would have collapsed. Anuli and Swati for giving me a home in Bombay while I was still figuring out what to do. Suzanna and Mervi for doing the same in New York.

Holly Mandel and the crew at Improvolution—my life would be bullshit without improv.

Brock Savage for directing 'Unladylike' the show, thank you for critiquing my writing, my performance and my skin. And to Or, Smi, and Davo for always being there to man the gates and party after.

Nadia Manzoor who is hell bent on getting me in trouble and

to the *Shugs & Fats* squad, we will make movies one day.

Katarina Kojic, without whom I would still be standing awkwardly around a camera. Plus I would not have this book cover.

Avni for being the baby that made me think I might want one and Ya for being the child that convinced me, beyond reasonable doubt, that motherhood was not for me.

Thaks for being patient, cool and manly. It is a great relief to be married to someone with hairier arms and an unending supply of faith in my abilities. And to my mum-in-law who is kind enough to keep pretending that I am a good Jat wife.

To all of you whose names I had to change because I haven't seen you in an age and I have no idea how we left it. And to those whose names I didn't change—I hope you know that you are amongst my favourite people so please don't sue me because I have no money.

Surya and Bertie Vaz. You are still weird. Every kid should be so lucky.

Made in the USA
Monee, IL
03 May 2026